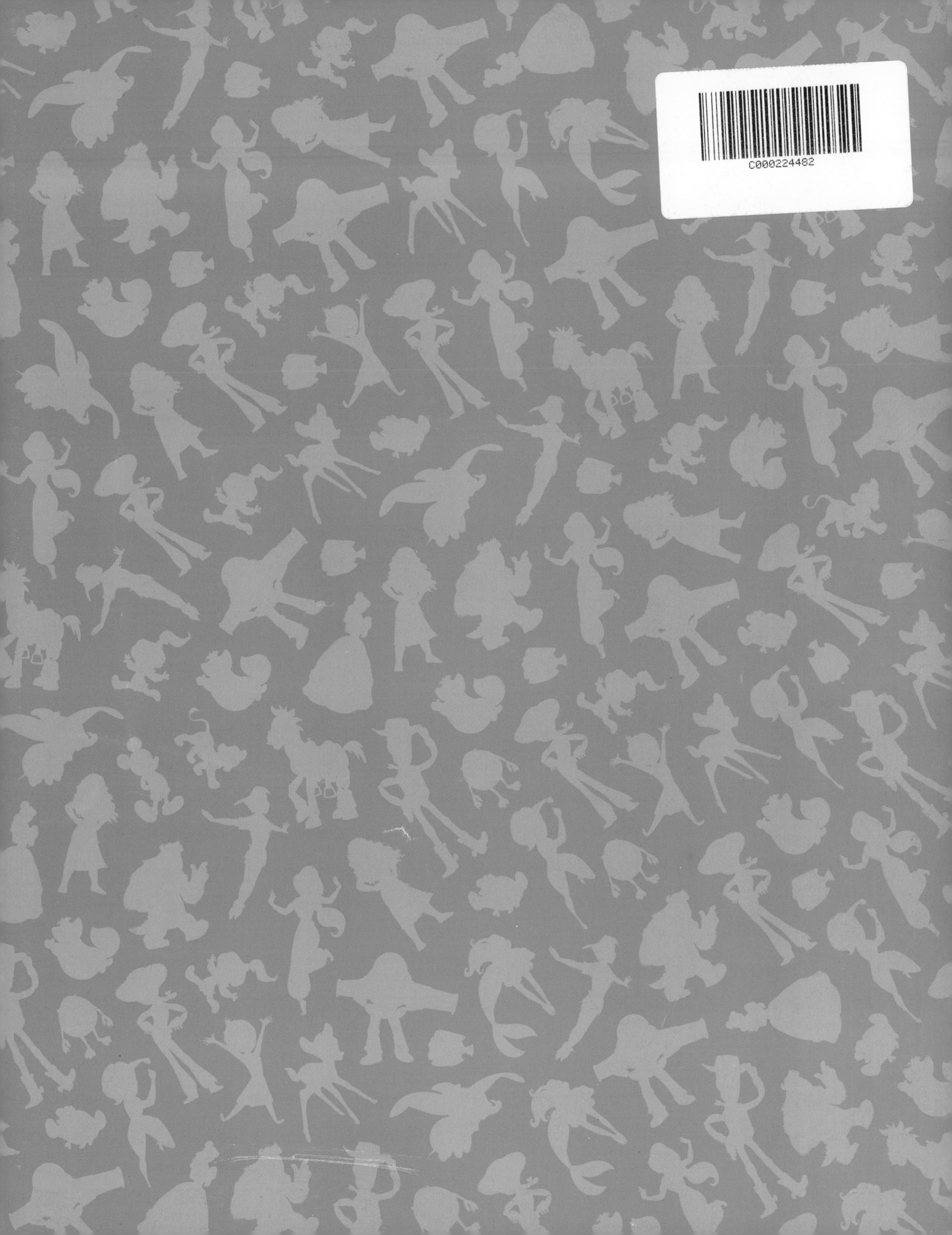

MY FIRST DISNEY PICTURE DICTIONARY

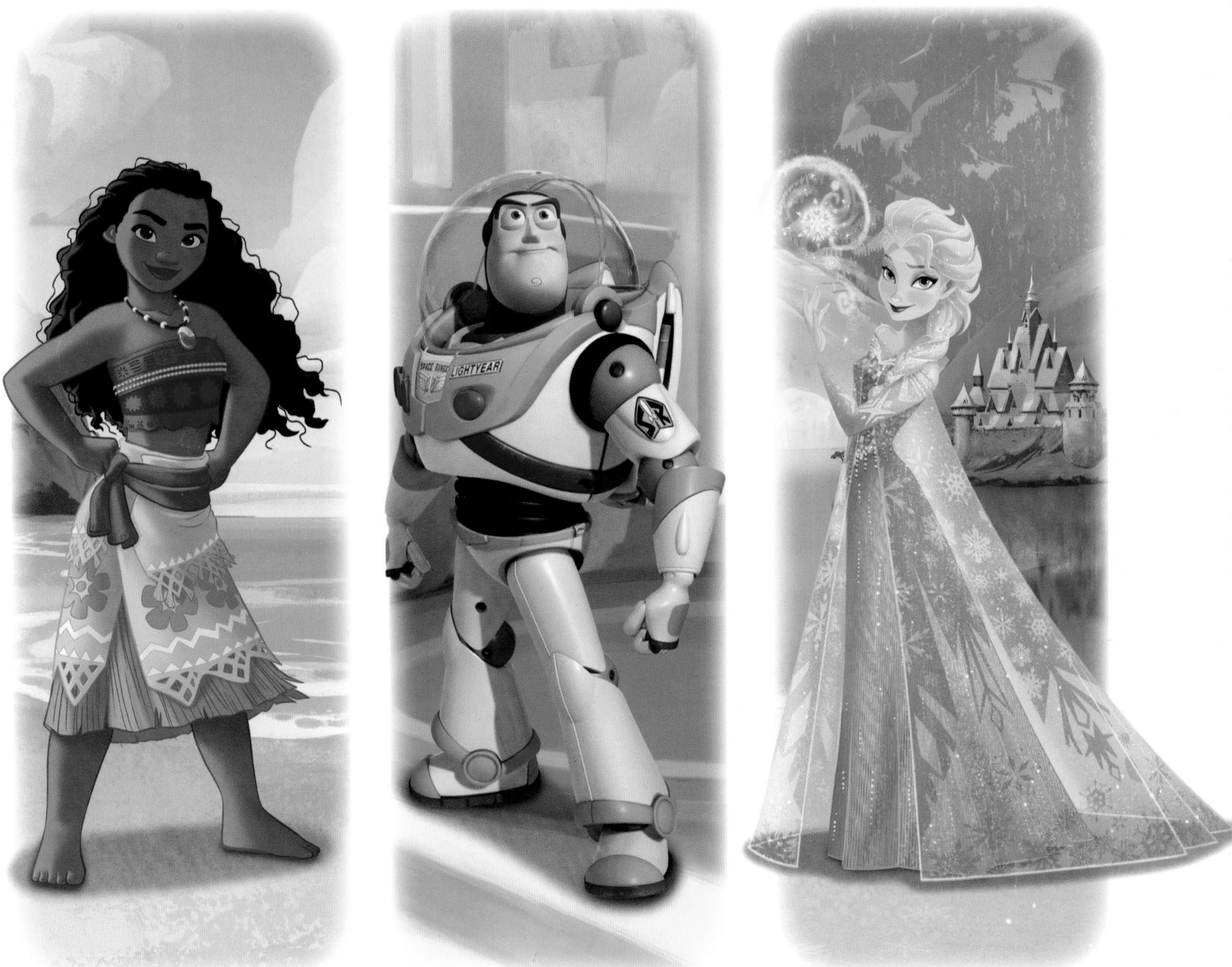

AUTUMN
PUBLISHING

Published in 2020
by Autumn Publishing
Cottage Farm
Sywell
NN6 0BJ

Autumn is an imprint of Bonnier Books UK

0520 001
2 4 6 8 10 9 7 5 3 1
ISBN 978-1-83903-108-3

Printed and manufactured in China

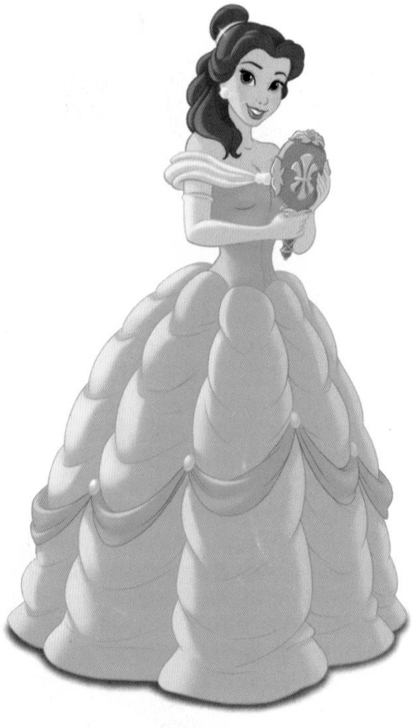

MY FIRST Disney PICTURE DICTIONARY

AUTUMN PUBLISHING

Aa

accident

An accident is something that happens by mistake.

Anna had an **accident** by falling from her horse.

acorn

An acorn is the hard nut of the oak tree.

Plant an **acorn** in the ground, then wait for it to grow into an oak tree.

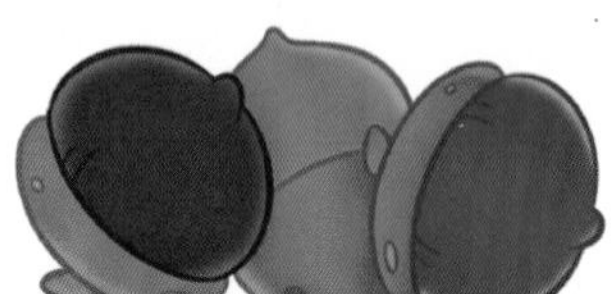

action

An action is something that is done.

Nick and Judy leap into **action**.

above

When you are above something, you are on top of it or higher than it.

Rafiki lifts Simba high **above** his head.

act

To act is to pretend to be something that you're not.

Mulan must **act** like a boy warrior.

actor

An actor is a person who pretends to be someone else in a film, a play or in a show on television.

Woody used to be an **actor** in a TV show.

add
When you add something, you put it with something else to make it bigger.

Flik wants to **add** to the colony's food store.

adventure
An adventure is something you do that is new and exciting.

Carl and Russell are going on a big **adventure**.

address
An address tells the location of a building or the place where someone lives. It can include a number, street, city, county and country.

Don't forget to write the **address** on this letter.

aeroplane
An aeroplane is a flying machine with wings that can carry people a long way.

An **aeroplane** is a speedy way to travel.

afternoon
Afternoon comes after 12 o'clock (midday).

Pooh likes to eat honey in the **afternoon**.

adult
An adult is someone who has grown up.

Dory's mum is an **adult** fish.

after
After means later than, or following.

Rapunzel and Eugene lived happily ever **after**.

age

Your age is how old you are.

Carl has reached an older **age** than Russell.

alien

An alien is a living creature from another planet.

To an **alien**, Earth seems like a curious place.

agree

When people agree, it means they think or feel the same way about something.

The animals **agree** that Snow White is sweet and kind.

all

All means every part of something.

All of the Pride Land animals are stampeding across the plain.

airport

An airport is a place where aeroplanes take off and land.

This **airport** has a runway in the middle.

alone

You are alone when you are by yourself.

The Beast sits **alone** in his castle.

alphabet

The alphabet is a list of all the letters you need to write words.

Can you remember all of the letters in the **alphabet**?

also

Also means as well as, in addition to.

As well as being creative, Rapunzel is **also** very active.

angry

When you get cross, you feel angry.

This looks like a very **angry** face!

answer

An answer is what you reply with after a question has been asked.

Mike is sure that he knows the right **answer**.

always

Always means all the time.

Dory is **always** ready to help a fish in need!

animal

An animal is any living thing that is not a plant.

Sven is an **animal** that lives in the mountains.

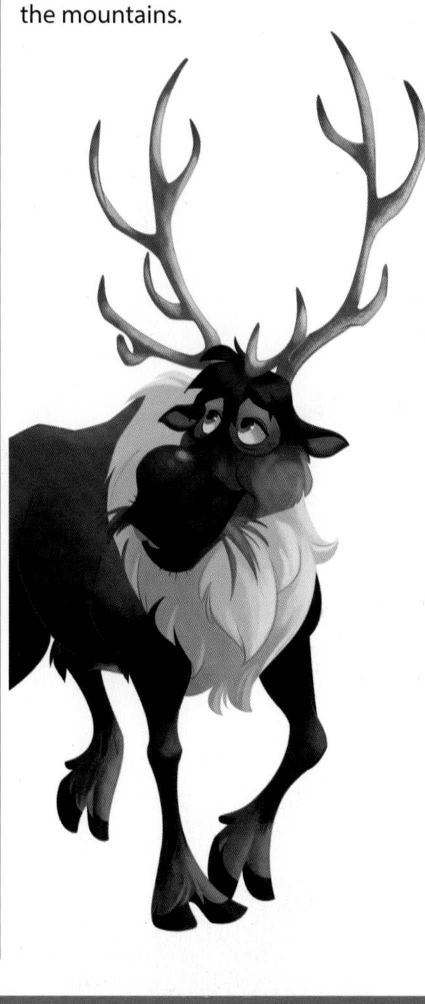

ant

An ant is a tiny, crawling insect that is very strong.

Atta is a royal **ant** princess.

ambulance

An ambulance is a van with a siren that takes ill or injured people to hospital.

Cars move to the side of the road to let an **ambulance** pass in an emergency.

apple

An apple is the fruit that grows on an apple tree.

Pinocchio has brought an **apple** for his teacher.

A B C D E F G H I J K L M N O P Q R S T U V W X Y Z

apron

An apron is something to wear that protects your clothing from getting dirty when you cook.

Friendly birds help Cinderella tie up her **apron**.

ask

When you ask something, you use words to form a question.

Aladdin wants to **ask** Jasmine to dance with him.

aunt

An aunt is your father or mother's sister, or your uncle's wife.

Hiro and Tadashi are in trouble with their **aunt**.

aquarium

An aquarium is a bowl or tank of water that holds fish and other sea creatures.

Gill and Nemo are trapped inside an **aquarium**.

astronaut

An astronaut is someone who travels into outer space.

Buzz Lightyear is a bold and fearless **astronaut**.

author

An author is a person who writes books, articles or documents.

Queen Elsa is the **author** of this letter.

around

Around means on all sides of something.

Kaa wraps his body **around** a log.

audience

An audience is a group of people watching something.

When Roger plays the piano, an **audience** appears!

autumn

Autumn is one of the four seasons of the year. It is when the leaves change colour and fall off the trees.

In **autumn**, the days get blustery.

Buzz Lightyear

Bb

baby

A baby is a very young child.

Moana is a **baby** with a special gift.

baboon

A baboon is a large monkey that lives in Africa.

Rafiki is a wise and kind-hearted **baboon**.

bacon

Bacon is salted and smoked meat that is sliced and fried.

Do you like the smell of **bacon** when it is cooking?

bad

When something is bad, it is naughty or not good.

Jafar may pretend to be good, but his heart is **bad**.

badminton

Badminton is a game played by hitting a shuttlecock over a net using rackets.

A game of **badminton** can be lots of fun!

bag

A bag is a soft container used to carry things.

What has Duke Weaselton got in his **bag**?

bake

When you bake something, you cook it in an oven.

Rapunzel can **bake** and decorate all sorts of tasty treats!

bakery

A bakery is a place that sells tasty food such as bread, cakes and biscuits.

Queen Elsa is visiting the **bakery**.

ball

A ball is a round object that is used to play games.

Joy is balancing and juggling on a **ball**.

balloon

A balloon is a thin rubber bag that is blown up with air or gas.

Young Carl is holding a **balloon** on a string.

band

A band is a group of musicians who play together.

This **band** makes everyone tap their feet along to Prince Naveen's singing!

bandage

A bandage is a strip of cloth used to cover a wound.

If you scrape your knee, cover it with a **bandage**.

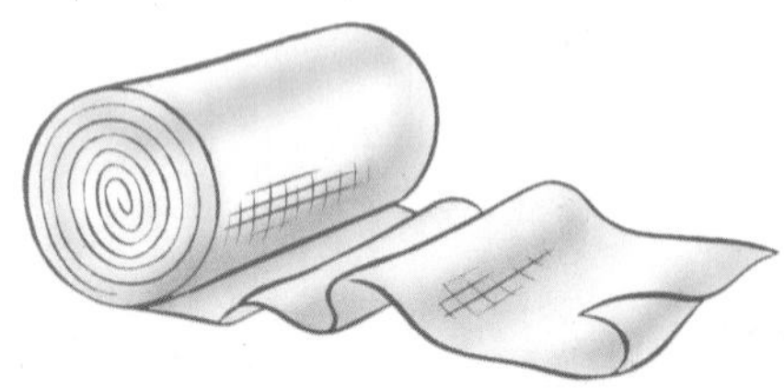

ballerina

A ballerina is a female ballet dancer.

Minnie Mouse is dancing like a **ballerina**.

banana

A banana is a long, yellow curved fruit that grows on a tree.

King Louie can eat a **banana** at any time of the day!

bank

A bank is a place where people keep their money safe.

The lemmings are leaving the **bank**.

bat (sports)

A bat is a stick used to hit a ball.

When it's your turn, swing the **bat** to hit the ball.

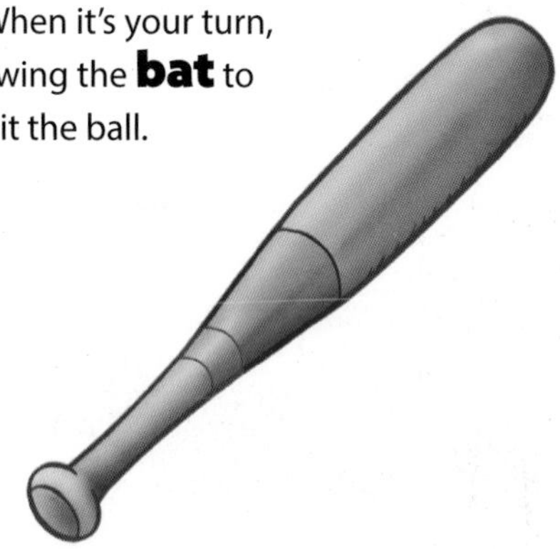

barbecue

A barbecue is a social gathering where food is cooked on a grill outdoors.

Mickey is treating his nephews to a **barbecue**!

basketball

Basketball is a game where you throw a large round ball through a raised hoop.

A **basketball** is good for bouncing on the ground.

bat (animal)

A bat is a flying animal that comes out at night.

A **bat** will hang upside down to sleep.

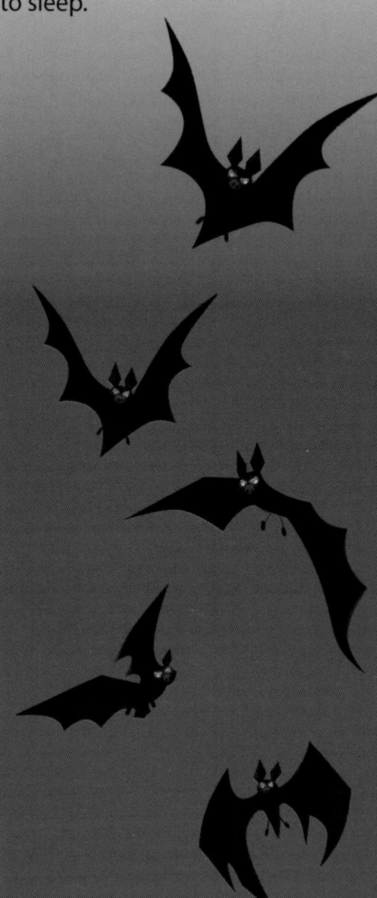

barn

A barn is a building where farm animals live.

Cows and horses can live in a **barn**.

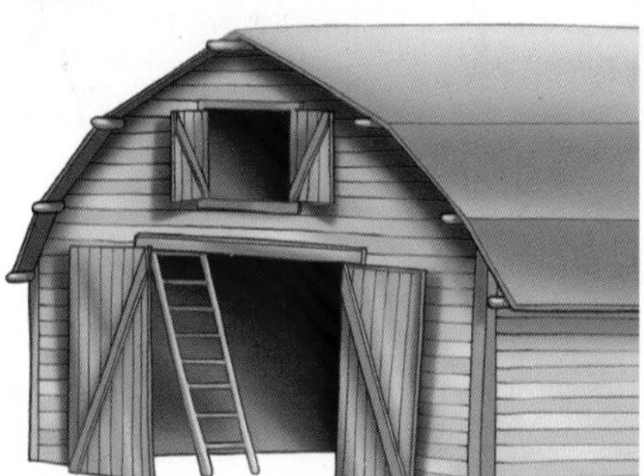

bass

The bass is the biggest instrument in an orchestra's string section.

A **bass** has strings that can be plucked.

bath

A bath is the container in which you wash yourself to get clean.

This **bath** is ready to be filled up with water.

bauble

A bauble is a decoration you hang on your Christmas tree.

Jaq is showing Cinderella and Prince Charming his favourite **bauble**.

bathrobe

A bathrobe is a piece of clothing that you put on after bathtime.

Snuggle up in your warm, comfy **bathrobe**.

be

To be is to live or exist.

Simba will **be** king someday.

beans

Beans are the seeds of different plants.

Beans come in lots of shapes and colours.

bathroom

A bathroom is a room with a sink, bath and often a shower and toilet.

Goofy loves singing in the **bathroom**.

beach

A beach is the sandy or rocky place at the edge of the sea.

The **beach** is where the ocean meets the land.

bear

A bear is a big, furry animal that growls when it talks and has sharp teeth and claws.

Merida's mother was transformed into a **bear**.

beard

A beard is the hair that grows on a man's chin and cheeks.

The Sultan has a bushy, white **beard**.

beautiful

Something beautiful is pleasing to look at.

Belle looks **beautiful** in her yellow ballgown.

become

Become means to change or grow into something new.

Ariel wants to **become** a human girl.

bed

A bed is a piece of furniture that you sleep on.

Pooh is happy to get into **bed** after a long, busy day!

bedroom

A bedroom is where you go to sleep at night.

Mickey shares a **bedroom** with his dog, Pluto.

bee

A bee is a flying insect that lives in a hive.

A **bee** collects pollen from flowers.

A B C D E F G H I J K L M N O P Q R S T U V W X Y Z

A B C D E F G H I J K L M N O P Q R S T U V W X Y Z

before

Before means earlier than something else.

The cars line up **before** the big race.

below

Below means under or lower than something else.

Dory swims **below** the stingrays.

berry

A berry is a small fruit that doesn't have a stone in the centre.

There are several different types of **berry**.

behind

Behind means at the back of something.

Bambi slides along **behind** Thumper.

belt

A belt is a long, narrow strip of leather or cloth that you wear around your waist.

Minnie has a new **belt** to go with her red dress.

best

If something is the best, it means that there is nothing else better.

Merida is the **best** archer in the clan.

bell

A bell is a hollow metal object that rings when it is struck.

The **bell** rings every morning when school starts.

bench

A bench is a narrow seat, often found in parks.

A **bench** is a good place to sit and enjoy some fresh air!

between

To be between something means to be in the middle of other things.

Alice is sitting **between** the Mad Hatter and the March Hare.

bicycle

A bicycle is something with two wheels, a seat and handlebars; you ride it by pushing on the pedals with your feet.

Goofy likes to ride his **bicycle** up and down hills.

birthday

Your birthday is a celebration of the day that you were born.

Mickey's friends have planned a **birthday** surprise!

bite

When you bite, you use your teeth to take hold or cut into something.

Lady tries to tug and **bite** on the tablecloth.

big

If something is big, it means it takes up a lot of space.

Poppa Henry is a **big** and heavy dinosaur.

blanket

A blanket is a soft cover that keeps you warm.

Belle has got a **blanket** to keep her knees warm.

bird

A bird is an animal that has wings and feathers, and lays eggs.

A peacock is a **bird** with colourful tail feathers.

biscuit

A biscuit is a sweet, baked snack made with flour, sugar, butter and other ingredients.

Would you like to take a **biscuit** from this tray?

blind

A person who is blind is unable to see.

Mama Odie is **blind** but has a snake as a guide.

boat

A boat carries people and things across water.

Mickey and Minnie are floating in a **boat**.

bone

Bones are the hard parts of a body that all together make up a skeleton.

Miguel is a little alarmed he can see his finger **bone**!

book

A book is something that you read. It has pages and a cover.

Belle's **book** is filled with stories.

body

Your body is all of you, inside and outside.

Your **body** has lots of different parts.

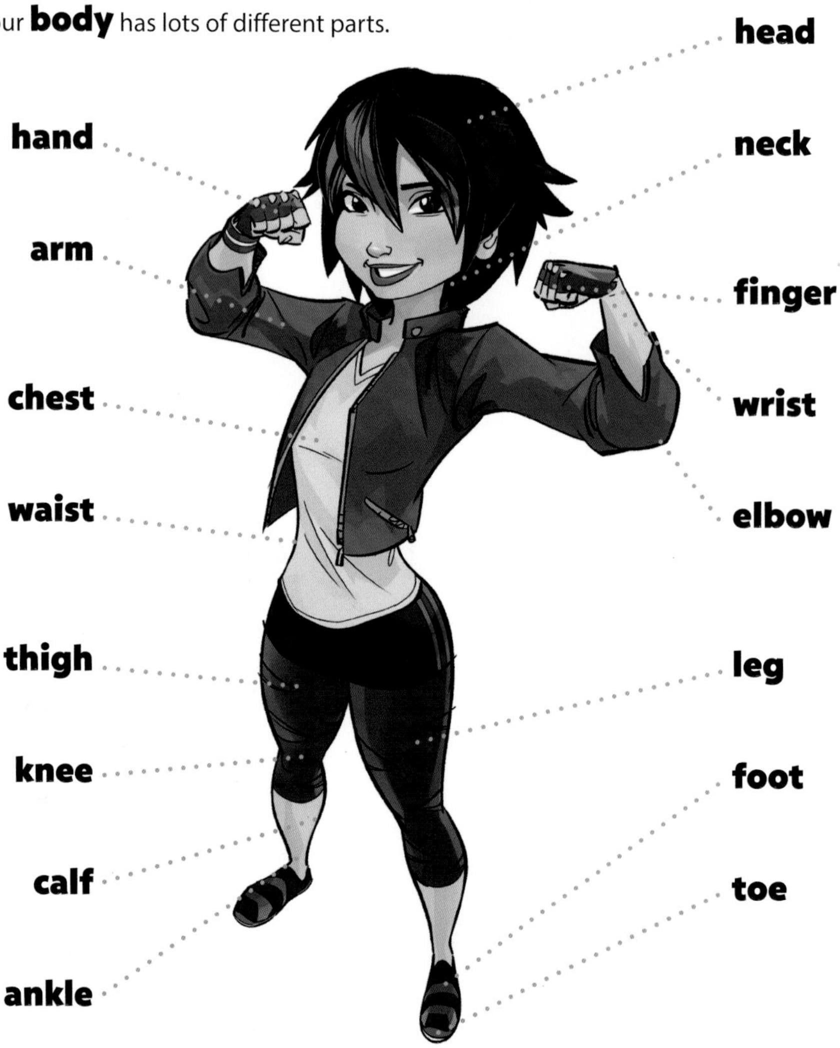

bookcase

A bookcase is a piece of furniture with shelves where you store books.

Belle's **bookcase** is very messy!

bookshop

A bookshop is a shop that sells books.

Rapunzel peeps into the **bookshop** window.

boots

Boots are shoes that cover part of the legs.

Woody wears a smart pair of cowboy **boots**.

bottle

A bottle is a container that holds liquid.

Judy is staring into a glass **bottle**.

bowl

A bowl is a deep, round dish that holds food.

This **bowl** is full of delicious fruit.

bored

You are bored when you have nothing interesting to do.

Carl gets **bored** with sitting in his armchair at home all day.

bottom

The bottom of something is the very lowest part of it.

Woody has got a name written on the **bottom** of his boot.

box

A box is a container usually in the shape of a square or rectangle.

The Queen has opened the wooden **box**.

boss

A boss is a person who is in charge.

Shenzi, Azizi and Kamari are a bit afraid of their **boss**, Scar!

bouncy

A bouncy object comes back up again when it hits the ground.

Tigger is very **bouncy** indeed!

boy

A boy is a male child who will grow up to be a man.

Hiro Hamada is a very clever **boy**.

bread

Bread is a food made from flour, water and yeast, and is baked.

This **bread** is crusty on the outside and soft on the inside.

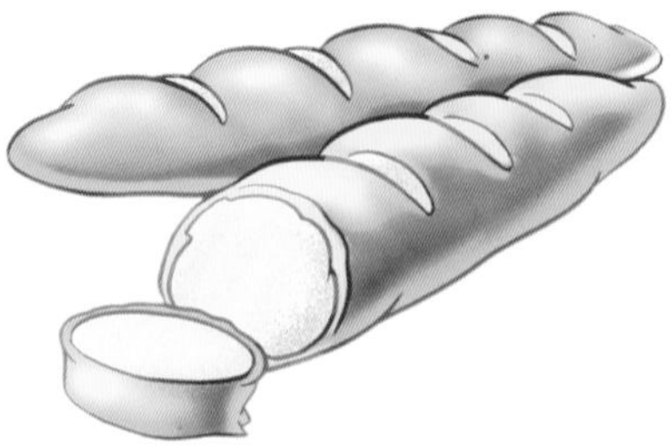

bridge

A bridge connects the gap between two pieces of land.

This **bridge** creaks and wobbles in the wind.

broccoli

Broccoli is a green vegetable that looks like a little tree.

Broccoli is very good for you.

break

When you break something, it falls to pieces or stops working.

Riley didn't mean to **break** her teddy bear.

broom

A broom is a long stick with a brush at the end of it that is used for sweeping.

Snow White uses her **broom** to sweep the Dwarfs' cottage.

breakfast

Breakfast is the first meal of the day.

Mickey and Pluto like to eat **breakfast** together.

bring

When you bring something, you take it with you when you go somewhere.

Rabbit needs to **bring** a lot of things over to Pooh's house.

brother
If you have a brother, he is the male child of your parents.

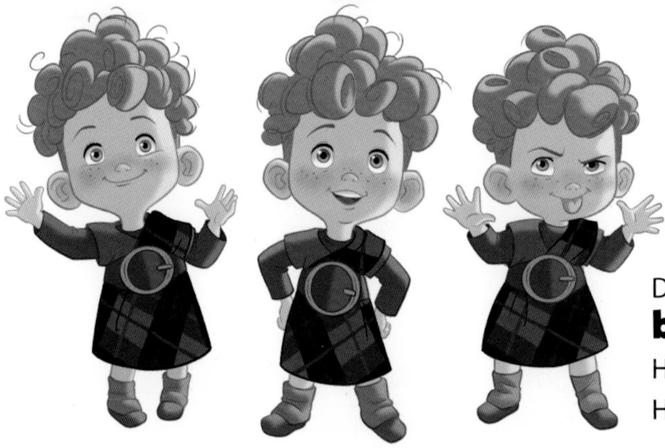

Do you have a cheeky **brother**, like Harris, Hubert and Hamish?

butterfly
A butterfly is a flying insect that has colourful wings.

A fluttery **butterfly** has landed on Dopey's nose!

bucket
A bucket is a container used to carry water, sand or other things.

Gerald likes to carry a **bucket** in his mouth.

bus
A bus is a long van that carries people from place to place. It has lots of seats and windows.

Mike is taking the **bus** home from Monsters University.

button
A button is a small round object that helps to fasten up clothes.

A **button** has holes in the middle.

building
A building is a place where people live or work. It has walls and a roof.

The palace in Agrabah is a very fine **building**.

butter
Butter is a soft food made from milk or cream.

There's a new block of **butter** in the dish.

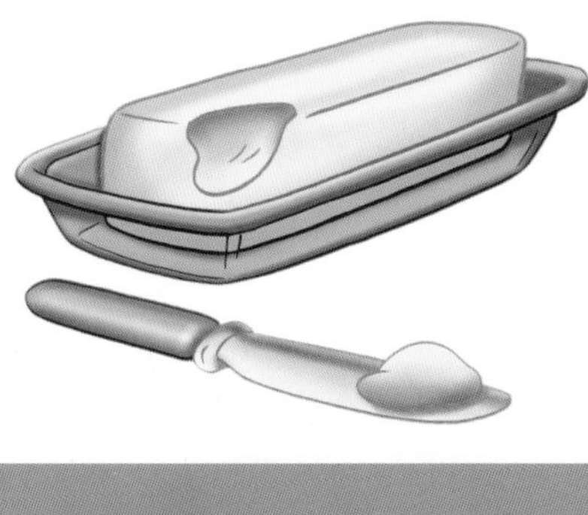

buy
When you buy something, you use money to pay for it so it can belong to you.

Anna and Elsa have come to **buy** a new pair of snowshoes.

Cruella De Vil

Cc

café

A café is a place that serves drinks and snacks such as sandwiches, cakes and juice.

It's nice to meet friends at a **café**.

cake

Cake is a sweet, baked dessert made with flour, sugar, butter and other ingredients.

Rapunzel has never seen such a grand **cake**!

calendar

A calendar lists all the days of the week, month and year.

A **calendar** helps us to remember important dates.

cabbage

Cabbage is a green vegetable that is cooked or eaten raw.

This **cabbage** has just been picked from the garden.

calculator

A calculator is a machine that can add, subtract, multiply and divide.

Lilo uses a **calculator** to work out tricky sums.

call

Call means to speak in a loud voice to get someone's attention, or to telephone someone.

Goofy is making a **call** to his friend, Mickey.

camel
A camel is an animal that lives in the desert and has one or two humps on its back.

This **camel** is searching for Aladdin.

camera
A camera is a machine that you use to take photographs.

This monster has put his **camera** on a tripod.

candle
A candle is a stick of wax with a wick that burns and gives out light.

It is getting dark, so Dopey lights a **candle**.

candlestick
A candlestick is a holder for a candle.

Lumière is an elegant brass **candlestick**.

candyfloss
Candyfloss is a sweet, tasty treat and is made out of spun sugar.

Bing Bong has a **candyfloss** body!

card
A card is a thick piece of paper, often with words and pictures on it.

Pick a **card**! Which one do you like best?!

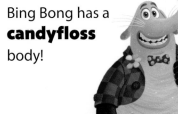

cardigan
A cardigan is a woolly piece of clothing that buttons up at the front.

When she's at work, Roz wears a dark red **cardigan**.

car
A car is a vehicle which usually has four wheels and an engine that is powered by petrol, diesel or electricity.

Lightning McQueen is the fastest **car** in town.

A B C D E F G H I J K L M N O P Q R S T U V W X Y Z

cards (playing)

Cards are thick pieces of rectangular paper, with different numbers and shapes on them, that are used for playing games.

Do you like playing **cards** on rainy days?

carry

When you carry something, you hold it to take it with you somewhere.

Judy Hopps can **carry** her bag in one hand.

cat

A cat is a pet that can purr and meow.

Lucifer is a mischievous and sneaky **cat**!

carpet

A carpet is a decorative covering for a floor.

Jasmine has never been on a flying **carpet** before!

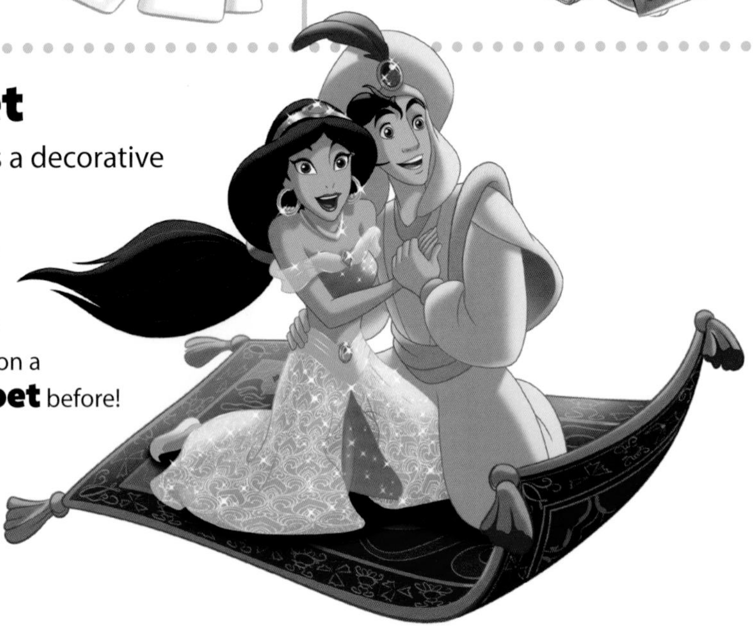

catch

When you catch something, you grab it as it is moving.

Mickey jumps up to **catch** the Frisbee.

carrot

A carrot is a vegetable that is the long, orange root of a carrot plant.

Rabbits love to eat a crunchy **carrot** or two.

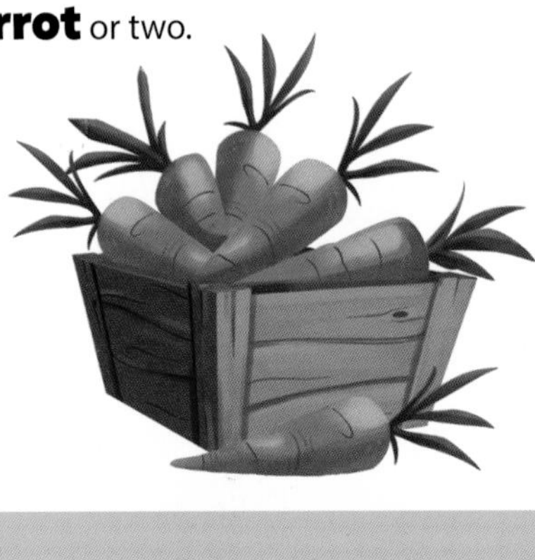

castle

A castle is a large building with thick, stone walls and tall towers.

A **castle** is a home for a royal princess.

caterpillar

A caterpillar is an insect that will turn into a butterfly or moth.

This **caterpillar** has a blue body and lots of legs.

cauliflower
A cauliflower is a large, round, bumpy-looking white vegetable.

A **cauliflower** is tasty and healthy, too.

cello
A cello is a musical instrument with strings that looks like a huge violin.

The top of this **cello** is taller than a chair.

chalk
Chalk is a stick of coloured powder that you can use for writing or drawing.

Water can wash away **chalk** marks.

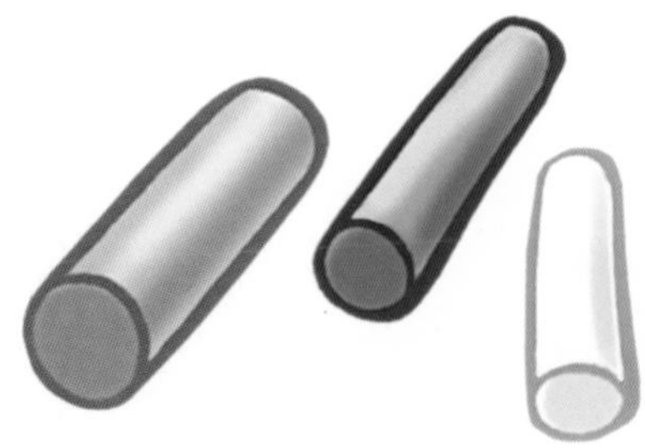

ceiling
The ceiling is the top part of a room.

The throne room at Arendelle castle has a very fine **ceiling**.

cereal
Cereal is a food you eat for breakfast.

Pour milk on your **cereal** before you eat it.

chameleon
A chameleon is a small reptile that can change colour.

Pascal the **chameleon** is great at hide-and-seek!

celery
Celery is a crunchy, stringy, green vegetable.

Celery makes a snapping sound when you break off a piece.

chair
A chair is a piece of furniture to sit on.

Cinderella sits on a **chair** to try on the glass slipper.

champion
A champion is the winner of a race, a game or a competition.

Lightning McQueen is the Piston Cup **champion**.

chase
When you chase something, you try to catch it.

Lady is playing **chase** with this bird.

chess
Chess is a game for two people, played with 32 pieces on a board with light and dark squares.

Queen Elinor is ready for a new game of **chess**.

children
Two or more young people are called children.

Anna and Elsa are very happy **children**.

cheese
Cheese is a food made from the milk of cows, sheep or goats.

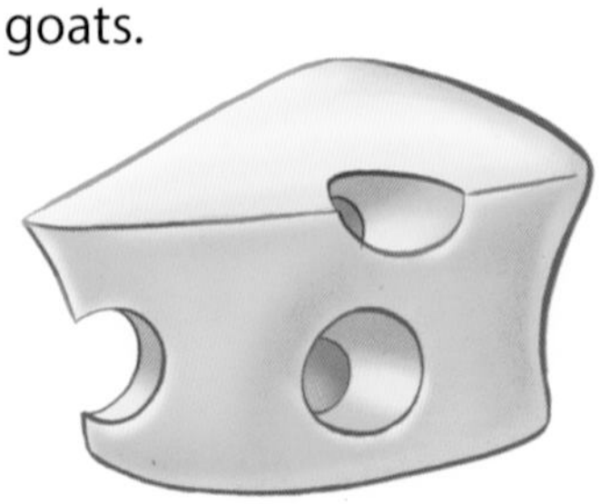

This piece of **cheese** has got holes in it!

chicken
A chicken is a bird that lays eggs. Chickens cluck after they lay an egg.

A **chicken** can only fly a short distance.

cherry
A cherry is the fruit that grows on a cherry tree.

A **cherry** is a feast to a little mouse like Jaq.

child
A child is a young person who will grow up to be an adult.

Spot is a **child** who lives in the wilderness.

chocolate
Chocolate is a sweet, brown treat made from cocoa beans and sugar.

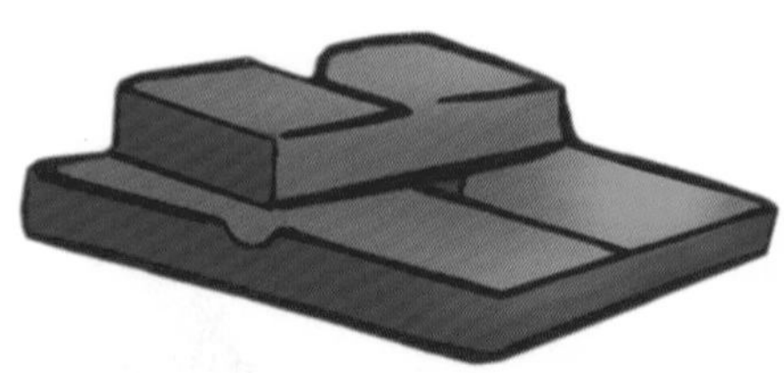

Unwrap a **chocolate** bar and take a big bite!

chopsticks

Chopsticks are narrow, pointy sticks that are used to pick up food.

Riley's mum likes eating with **chopsticks**.

clap

You clap your hands together to show you are pleased with something.

This trick deserves a **clap**!

clean

If something is clean, it is not dirty.

This enchanted dustpan will **clean** up the floor in no time!

choose

When you choose something, you pick it out from other things.

Mickey and his friends must **choose** what to eat.

classroom

A classroom is the room in a school where a teacher teaches students.

The monsters are sitting in their **classroom**.

climb

When you climb, you use your hands and feet to pull yourself up higher.

Moana and Maui **climb** up the mountain.

city

A city is a large town where lots of people live and work.

Zootropolis is a very busy **city**.

clock

A clock is a machine that tells the time.

This **clock** chimes every hour.

clown

A clown is a performer in a circus who wears funny clothes and does things to make people laugh.

This **clown** has a bright red nose and enormous shoes!

coffee

Coffee is a drink made from roasted coffee beans.

Lots of people drink **coffee** in the morning.

close

When you close something, such as a door, you shut it.

Sulley tries to **close** the door as quietly as he can.

coach

A coach is a person who teaches people how to do something better.

Mike is Sulley's scaring **coach**.

coin

A coin is a round, metal piece of money.

If you find a **coin**, keep it safe until it's time to go shopping.

cloud

A cloud is a white shape in the sky, made up of millions of tiny raindrops.

A **cloud** can be puffy and round, or long and wispy.

coat

A coat is a piece of clothing you wear over other clothes to keep warm and dry.

When it is cold, Christopher Robin buttons up his **coat**.

cold

When you have a cold, you sneeze a lot and you don't feel well.

Queen Elsa has got a bad **cold**. Atishoo!

colours

The way that objects reflect light makes them appear in different colours.

Rapunzel paints a picture using all of her favourite **colours**.

comb

A comb is a flat piece of wood or plastic with 'teeth' that you use to keep your hair neat.

A **comb** stops your hair from getting in a tangle.

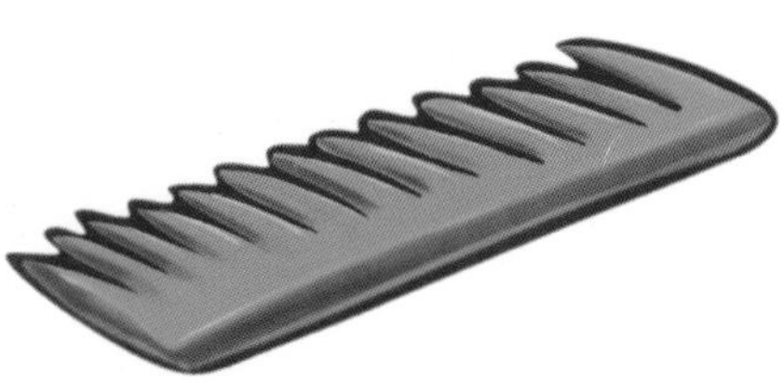

computer

A computer is a machine we type on and can complete tasks with, like writing letters.

Bellwether has a brand new **computer**.

concert

A concert is an event when musicians play for an audience.

The jazz **concert** was a thumping success!

A B C D E F G H I J K L M N O P Q R S T U V W X Y Z

cook

When you cook food, you heat it up by boiling, baking or frying it.

Robin Hood likes to **cook** outside.

cost

The cost of something is how much money is needed to buy it.

Mickey wants to know the **cost** of four tickets.

count

You count things to find out how many of them you have.

Uncle Scrooge loves to **count** his money.

corn

Corn is a vegetable with little rows of yellow seeds, that grows on a tall, green plant.

When **corn** is freshly picked, it still has green leaves on it.

costume

A costume is clothing you put on so that you will look like someone else.

Mike and Sulley are hiding Boo in a monster **costume**.

corner

A corner is where two walls or two streets come together.

Mike meets a friend on the **corner** of the street.

cough

When you cough, you try to clear your throat.

All that dust is making Goofy **cough**!

country

A country is a large area of land with its own laws and borders.

This map shows a **country** called Australia.

A B C D E F G H I J K L M N O P Q R S T U V W X Y Z

cousin
Your cousin is the child of your aunt and uncle.

Judy Hopps has got lots of bunny **cousins**.

crab
A crab is an animal that lives in the water. It has a shell, eight legs and two big claws.

Ariel is friends with a **crab** called Sebastian.

cricket
Cricket is a game played between two teams of eleven players. While one team tries to hit a ball with a bat to score 'runs', the other team tries to get them out.

Tigger can't wait to play his first **cricket** match in the Hundred-Acre Wood.

cow
A cow is a large farm animal that moos.

This **cow** is wearing a bell around its neck.

crackers
Crackers are thin, crispy snacks made of flour and water.

Crackers and cheese taste good together.

cowboy
A cowboy is someone who works on a special type of farm called a ranch and rides a horse.

Yee-ha! Woody is the best **cowboy** in the whole wide world!

crocodile
A crocodile is an animal that lives in water. It has short legs, tough skin and a long snout.

Louis is a **crocodile** that likes to play the trumpet.

crown

A crown is a round head ornament made of metal and jewels that kings and queens wear.

Prince John is trying to steal his brother's **crown**.

cry

When you cry, tears drip from your eyes because you are full of emotion.

When she thinks of home, Riley begins to **cry**.

cucumber

A cucumber is a vegetable with seeds, usually eaten raw in salads.

The best way to eat a **cucumber** is in slices.

cup

A cup is a container with a handle, that you drink from.

Chip Potts can make a lovely **cup** of tea!

cupboard

A cupboard is a cabinet with doors and shelves, where you store things.

Lots of dishes are kept inside this **cupboard**.

cushion

A cushion is a pillow on a chair or a sofa.

This sofa **cushion** is green and soft.

cut

When you cut something, you use a knife or a pair of scissors to divide it into parts.

Mickey likes to **cut** his apple into pieces.

cymbals

Cymbals are two big circles of metal that are banged together to make a loud musical sound.

These **cymbals** have straps to put your hands through.

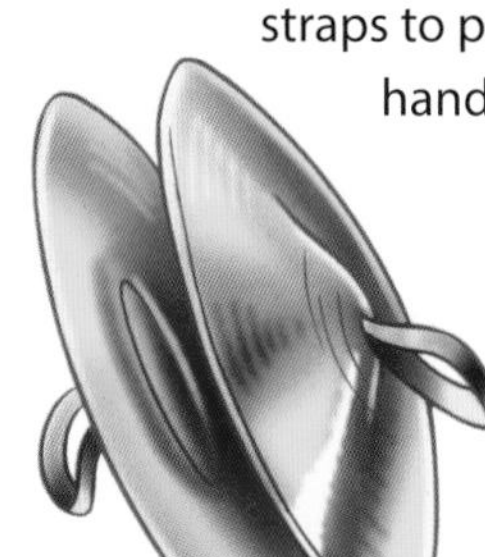

Dumbo

Dd

daughter
A daughter is a female person who has parents.

Bonnie and Stu Hopps love their **daughter** very much.

deer
A deer is an animal with four legs that lives in the forest. Young deer have spots on their fur.

This **deer** is Bambi, the Prince of the Forest!

day
A day is twenty-four hours long. Morning, afternoon and evening are part of one day.

Ariel spends all **day** looking for human treasure.

dentist
A dentist helps take care of your teeth.

This **dentist** has pulled out a large tooth!

dance
When you dance, you move your body to music.

Jaq and Gus like to **dance** for Cinderella.

deaf
A person who is deaf is unable to hear.

Mickey is trying to warn his friends that playing their music too loud might make them **deaf**!

department store
A department store has several sections selling different things.

Mickey and Minnie are shopping in the **department store**.

desert

A desert is a very hot, sandy, dry place.

The cars skid along the **desert** track.

desk

A desk is a piece of furniture used for writing and other kinds of work.

Merida is tired of sitting at her **desk**.

dessert

Dessert is a sweet food, usually eaten after dinner.

Find a spoon, then dig into this yummy **dessert**!

different

If something is different, it is not like other things.

Elsa has powers that make her **different** from her sister, Anna.

difficult

If something is difficult, it is hard to do or to understand.

Bambi thinks that walking on ice is very **difficult**.

dinner

Dinner is the last meal of the day.

Ariel is thrilled to have **dinner** with Prince Eric.

dinosaur

A dinosaur is an animal that roamed the Earth millions of years ago.

Arlo tries his hardest to be a big, brave **dinosaur**.

dirty

When something is dirty, it is not clean.

Snow White has never seen so many **dirty** dishes!

disagree

If you disagree with somebody, you each have different ideas about something.

Rapunzel and Mother Gothel **disagree** on everything!

dishes

Dishes are used to hold food.

Where do you keep the **dishes** in your house?

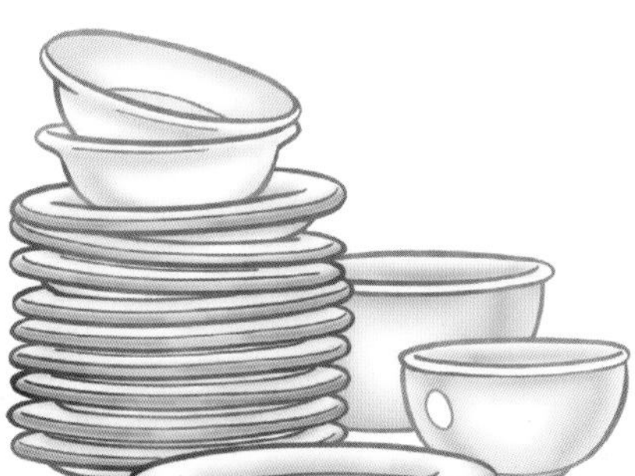

dishwasher

A dishwasher is a machine that washes dishes.

The **dishwasher** makes the dirty dishes nice and clean!

diving

Diving is when you jump head first into a pool. It is also short for scuba diving, when you go deep underwater with a tank that helps you to breathe.

Sometimes humans go **diving** in Nemo's reef.

DJ

A DJ is someone who chooses music to play on the radio or at dance events.

This **DJ** is playing some great tunes!

doctor

A doctor helps to make you better when you're sick.

Abigail needs to see a **doctor**.

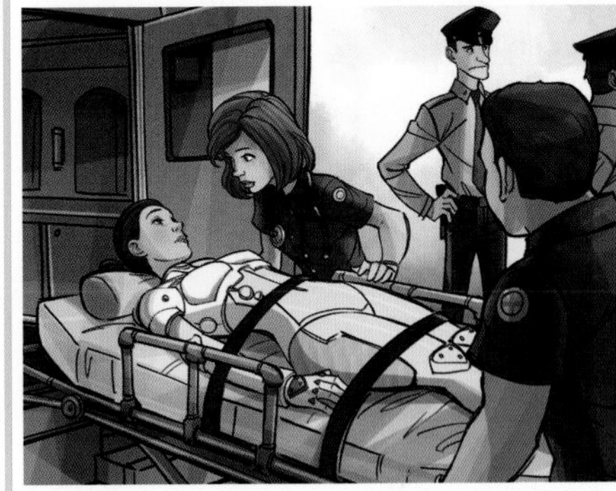

dog

A dog is a pet that barks and wags its tail when it's happy.

Pongo is a spotty Dalmatian **dog**.

doll

A doll is a toy that looks like a person.

A **doll** is always ready to be your friend!

A B C D E F G H I J K L M N O P Q R S T U V W X Y Z

A B C D E F G H I J K L M N O P Q R S T U V W X Y Z

dolphin

A dolphin is a very smart, small whale that lives in the sea and is friendly to people.

Would you like to swim with a **dolphin**?

down

When something is down, it is in a low place.

Oaken's trading post is **down** at the bottom of this slope.

door

You open and close a door to get in and out of a room or building.

Winnie the Pooh is waiting outside the **door**.

drawer

A drawer is part of a piece of furniture that slides in and out and holds things.

The top **drawer** is overflowing with clothes!

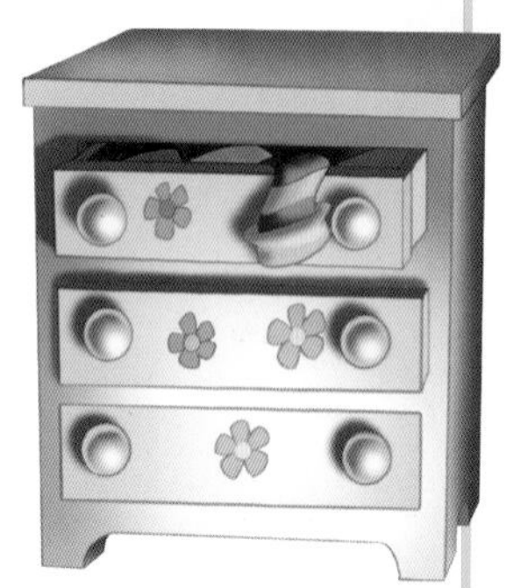

doorbell

A doorbell is outside a house. When you press it, it rings to let people know you are there.

Minnie presses the **doorbell** and Daisy answers!

draw

When you draw, you make pictures with a pencil, pen, crayon or chalk.

Rapunzel used a pencil to **draw** this picture of Maximus.

dream

Dreams are the images and thoughts you have when you sleep.

Alice and Dinah are having a lovely **dream**.

dress

A dress is a top and a skirt joined together as one piece.

Cinderella is very proud of her sparkly **dress**.

drive

When you are old enough to drive, you will be able to control a vehicle like a car or truck.

Mickey is going to **drive** his friends to the seaside.

dry

When something is dry, it does not have any liquid on it.

Simba stays **dry** by riding on Pumbaa.

drop

When you drop something, you let it fall.

Moana lets the shell **drop** into the water.

duck

A duck is a flying bird that quacks and likes to live and swim in water.

This mother **duck** has got two little ducklings.

drink

A drink is a liquid you swallow so you are no longer thirsty.

Terri and Terry do not like to **drink** the same thing.

drum

A drum is a round musical instrument that you bang on with sticks to make a sound.

A **drum** is used to set the beat to a tune.

DVD

A DVD is a disc that enables you to watch a film or TV programme whenever you want on a DVD player or computer.

Shall we sit down and watch a **DVD**?

A
B
C
D
E
F
G
H
I
J
K
L
M
N
O
P
Q
R
S
T
U
V
W
X
Y
Z

Ee

Earth

Earth is the name of the planet you live on.

From space, **Earth** looks like a giant marble.

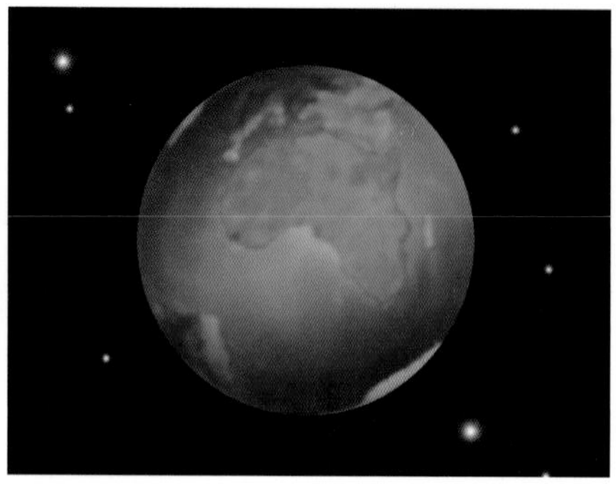

easy

If something is easy, it means it is not hard to do.

Swimming is **easy** for Ariel and Flounder!

east

East is the opposite direction of west.

The sun rises in the **east** every morning.

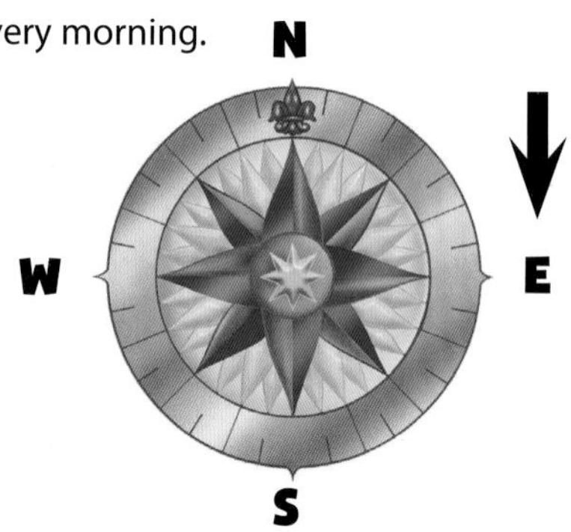

eat

When you eat, you take food into your mouth, then chew it and swallow it.

Mulan and her family are ready to **eat** their dinner.

early

Early means before the usual time.

When it comes to Monsters University, Mike is **early** for everything!

egg

Eggs are oval objects in which some baby animals grow until they are ready to be born.

There is a baby dinosaur inside this **egg**.

elephant

An elephant is a large animal with big ears and a long nose called a trunk.

Dumbo is an **elephant** with huge ears!

environment

Your environment is everything around you, including the trees, the clouds and the animals.

The jungle is an exciting **environment** for a human boy.

e-mail

E-mail is the kind of mail you get through your computer or smartphone.

Hiro is waiting for an important **e-mail**.

entrance

An entrance is the opening you go through to get inside a building.

King Fergus is hiding behind this **entrance**.

empty

Empty means that there is nothing inside.

The dog basket is **empty**.

envelope

An envelope is a flat paper container used to put a letter inside.

Will Snow White's next letter need a big or small **envelope**?

escalator

An escalator is a moving stairway that takes you up or down from floor to floor.

Donald and Daisy ride up the **escalator**.

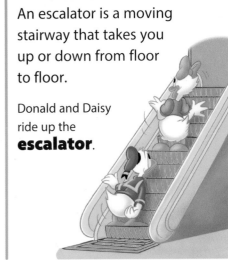

evening

Evening is the early part of the night.

Tiana and her family spend the **evening** on the porch.

excited

You feel excited when you are waiting for something or doing something that makes you happy.

Olaf feels **excited** most of the time!

exit

An exit is the opening you go through to leave a building.

A clan of angry men storm out of the **exit**.

everyone

Everyone means each and every person.

Everyone wants Snow White to stay at the cottage.

everything

Everything means all things.

Everything in here is made of gold.

exercise

When you exercise, you are doing activities that help your body stay fit and healthy.

Donald does some **exercise** every single day.

explorer

An explorer is someone who goes to unknown places to find out what they are like.

Carl's friend, Ellie, has always wanted to be an **explorer**.

Flounder

Ff

fairy

A fairy is a magical creature with wings which takes on a human form.

Flora is one of Aurora's three **fairy** godmothers.

fall

When things fall, they drop from a higher place to a lower place.

Oh no! Mickey and Minnie are going to **fall** in!

face

Your face is the front part of your head that includes your eyes, nose and mouth.

Merida's **face** glows when she's out in the fresh air.

family

A family is a group of people that are related to each other.

Merida and her **family** always eat dinner together.

father

Your father is your parent who is a man.

Tiana's **father** is very proud of his little girl.

fan

A fan is a machine that moves air around to make you feel cooler.

This **fan** sits on a desk or a table.

farm

A farm is a piece of land used for growing food and keeping animals.

This **farm** is in the countryside.

feather

A feather is a part of a bird that helps it fly and keeps it warm.

Each **feather** on a bird is delicate and light.

far

If something is far from you, it is a long distance away.

From this rock, Spot can see **far** into the distance.

fast

When something is fast, it happens quickly.

Vanellope's go-kart is **fast** and furious!

feel

When you feel something, you touch it or it touches you.

Can you **feel** Rapunzel tickling you, Pascal?

fence

A fence is an outdoor wall, usually made out of wood, separating two places.

An angry chicken chases Pluto through the **fence**.

film

A film is a story told in moving pictures, then shown on a screen.

Carl is watching a black and white **film**.

firefighter

It's a firefighter's job to put out fires.

Brave **firefighter** planes drop water on the flames.

field

A field is a flat, open piece of land without buildings.

In this **field**, Bambi can run free.

finish

To finish something is to come to the end of it.

Piglet has decided to **finish** painting Pooh.

fireworks

When lit, fireworks make loud noises and create beautiful, bright lights in the sky.

Bright **fireworks** shimmer above the ship.

fight

A fight is an argument between people.

Violet and Dash are having another **fight**!

fire

Fire describes the heat, flames and light that result when something burns.

Moana uses **fire** to light up the darkness.

A
B
C
D
E
F
G
H
I
J
K
L
M
N
O
P
Q
R
S
T
U
V
W
X
Y
Z

first

When something comes first, it comes before anything else.

Which plane will come **first** in the race?

fix

To fix something is to mend it when it is broken.

Mickey has tried to **fix** the sink!

floor

A floor is the part of a room that you walk on.

Joy draws a circle on the **floor**.

first-aid kit

A first-aid kit is a container that holds things to treat an injury or sickness.

It's a good idea to have a **first-aid kit** in the house.

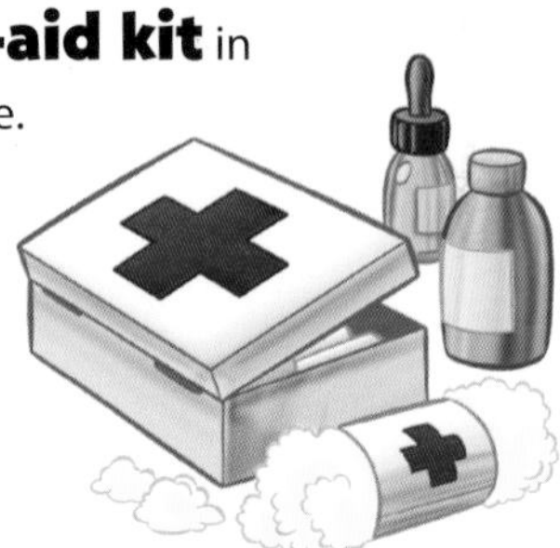

flag

A flag is a piece of cloth with a coloured design or pattern on it.

Every **flag** in this parade is bright and cheerful.

fish

A fish is an animal with fins that lives in the water and breathes through gills.

Dory is a **fish** who finds it hard to remember things.

float

To float means to stay on top of the water and not sink.

Mickey and his friends like to **float** for hours on end.

flour

Flour is a powder you use in baking.

You need two scoops of **flour** for the cake that you are making.

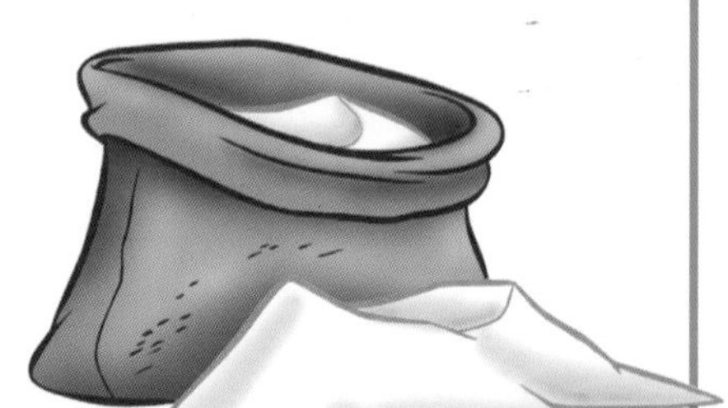

flower

A flower is the colourful part of a plant that has petals and contains seeds.

Every **flower** in this vase smells delightful!

fly (movement)

To fly means to move through the air.

No other robot can **fly** as high as Baymax.

follow

When you follow something, you go after it or behind it.

All of the Lost Boys **follow** after John.

flute

A flute is a musical instrument shaped like a long tube, which you hold sideways and play by blowing into the hole at one end.

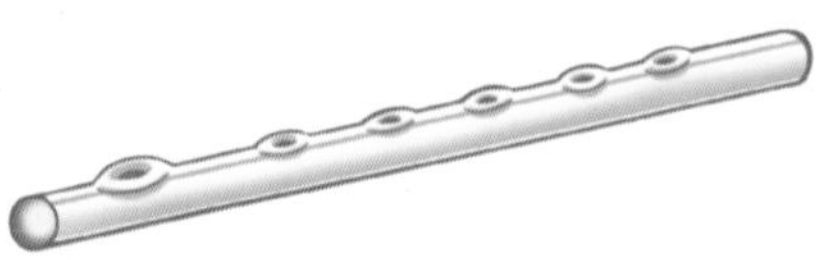

A **flute** can make high sounds.

fog

Fog is a thick cloud of mist that can be difficult to see through.

There is so much **fog**, Dusty has lost his way.

football

Football is a game played by two teams, where each team tries to kick a ball into the other team's goal.

Mickey and Goofy love to play **football** together.

fly (insect)

A fly is an insect with one set of clear wings.

This **fly** is buzzing about, looking for food.

fold

When you fold something, you bend one part over another.

Let's **fold** this piece of paper in half.

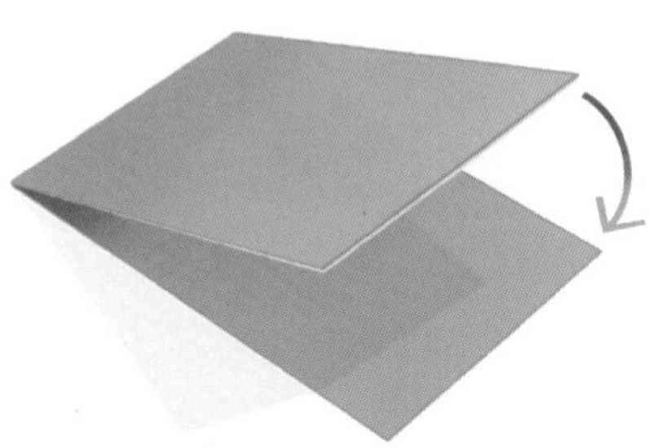

footprint

A footprint is the mark that a foot or a shoe makes on the ground.

Pooh wonders who would make a **footprint** like this?

fork

A fork is a tool that you use when you eat. It has long, pointy prongs and a handle.

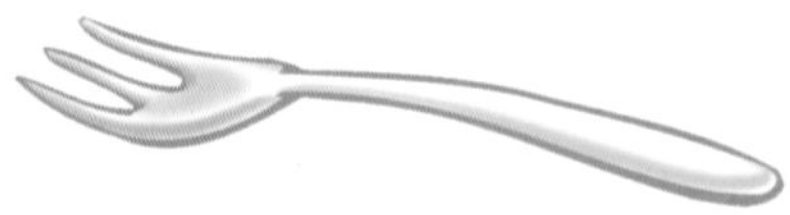

You can use a **fork** to pick up your food.

free

Something is free if it costs nothing.

These puppies aren't for sale, they're **free**!

forest

A forest is a place filled with trees growing very close together.

There are will o' the wisps in this **forest**.

fountain

A fountain is a jet of water that shoots up in the air and comes down in pretty streams.

This **fountain** makes a gentle, bubbling noise.

freeze

Water freezes when it gets so cold that it turns to ice.

The winter air has made this fountain **freeze**.

forget

When you forget something, you cannot remember it.

Try not to **forget**, Dory!

fox

A fox is an animal with orange or red fur, a pointy nose and a bushy tail.

Nick Wilde is a **fox** who is never far from trouble.

friend

A friend is someone you like and have fun and spend time with.

Woody and Buzz love their good **friend**, Hamm.

fur

Fur is the thick hair on many animals.

Sulley has a coat of fluffy blue and purple **fur**.

frog

A frog is a hopping animal with slimy skin that says "ribbit".

Could this **frog** really be a handsome prince?

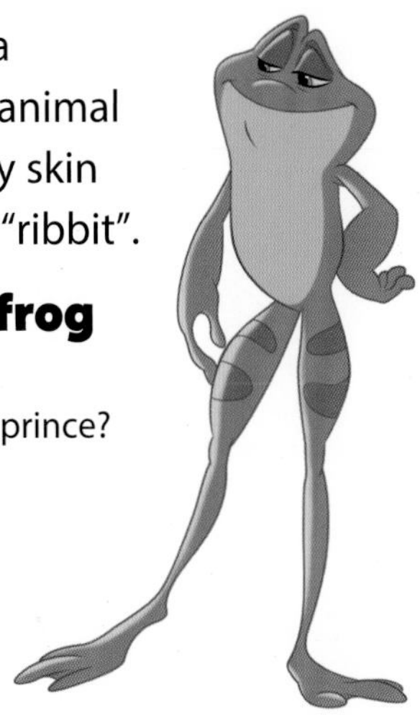

fruit

A fruit is something that grows on trees or plants, has seeds and is tasty to eat.

Fruit salad makes a tasty teatime treat.

furniture

Pieces of furniture are large objects in a house, such as tables, chairs, cupboards and beds.

What **furniture** do you have in your bedroom?

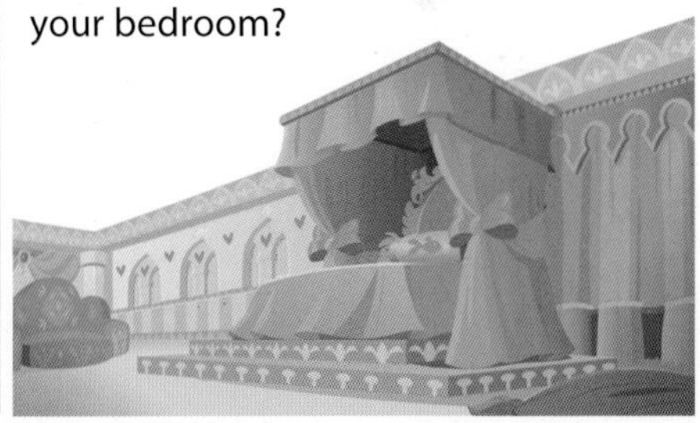

frown

A frown is the look on a person's face when he or she is unhappy and the ends of their mouth turn down.

The Queen of Hearts is wearing an angry **frown**.

full

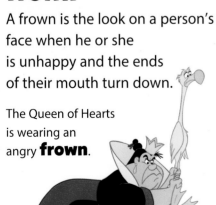

Full means that there is no room for anything else.

This car is packed **full** of monsters!

Grumpy

Gg

game
A game is something that you play, either on your own or as part of a team.

Riley is playing a **game** of ice hockey.

garage
A garage is a building where one or more vehicles are parked.

Doc finds Lightning parked in his **garage**.

garden
A garden is a spot where people grow flowers, vegetables and other plants.

This **garden** looks so pretty when the sun shines.

genie
A genie is a spirit who usually lives in a magic lamp and can make wishes come true.

When Aladdin rubs the lamp, a **genie** rushes out!

get
To get something is to have it by borrowing it, buying it or receiving it from someone else.

Kristoff went to **get** a present for Anna.

ghost
A ghost is thought to be the spirit of someone who has died.

A **ghost** has come to spook Uncle Scrooge!

giraffe
A giraffe is a very tall, spotted animal with long, thin legs and a very long neck.

A **giraffe** uses its long neck to reach the leaves on tall trees.

girl
A girl is a female child who will grow up to become a woman.

Alice is a sweet and dreamy **girl**.

give
When you give to someone, you let them have something.

Scrooge wants to **give** gifts to all of his friends!

glass
A glass is a container that we drink from.

This **glass** is empty.

glasses
Glasses are frames with special glass in them that you wear over your eyes when you need to see better.

Carl needs **glasses** to look at his photo album.

globe
A globe is a ball-shaped map of the world.

A **globe** shows land and the ocean, too.

A B C D E F G H I J K L M N O P Q R S T U V W X Y Z

glove

A glove is a piece of clothing that covers each finger of your hand separately to keep you warm or clean.

You can wriggle your fingers in your **glove**!

goal

In some sports, a goal is the place where you try to get the ball in order to score points.

Goal! Donald kicked the ball into the **goal**.

glue

Glue is a gooey liquid that lets us stick one thing to another.

Glue can get messy if you leave the lid off.

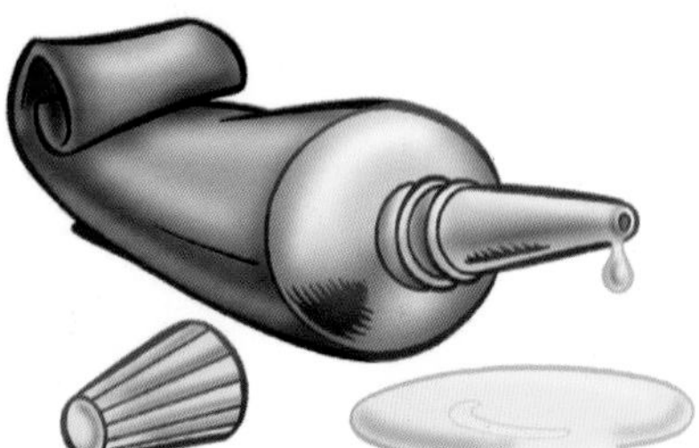

goldfish

A goldfish is a small, orange fish that many people keep as a pet.

Goldfish can live in a fishbowl, a tank or a pond.

good

Something that we like or that is done well is good.

Wee Dingwall fired a **good** shot.

go

To go means to move from one place to another.

Vanellope and her kart are ready to **go**!

gorilla

A gorilla is a large and strong wild animal that comes from Africa.

A **gorilla** bangs on its chest to tell everyone that it has arrived.

grandchildren

When you grow up, the children of your son or daughter will be your grandchildren.

Some grandmas tell stories to their **grandchildren**.

grapes

Grapes are small, round fruit that grow in bunches on a vine.

Do these **grapes** look tasty?

guitar

A guitar is a musical instrument played by plucking or strumming the strings with your fingers.

Rapunzel can rock a tune on the **guitar**!

grandparent

Your grandparent is the parent of your own parent.

Tala is a wise and generous **grandparent**.

grass

Grass is a plant with short green blades that cover the ground.

Rapunzel is happy to sit on the **grass** and sing.

gymnastics

Gymnastics are exercises that show how strong, bendy, well-balanced or fit you are.

Goofy and Mickey are learning to do **gymnastics**.

grapefruit

A grapefruit is a big, round, juicy fruit that grows on a tree.

Some **grapefruit** are yellow and some are pink.

guess

When you guess something, you say what you think is the correct thing, but you aren't sure if it's the right answer.

Will anyone **guess** that Mulan is really a girl?

A B C D E F G H I J K L M N O P Q R S T U V W X Y Z

Hiro

Hh

hair

Hair is made up of thin, thread-like strands which grow on your head and body.

Rapunzel's golden **hair** tumbles all the way down to the floor.

hairbrush

A hairbrush is a brush that you use to make your hair neat and tidy.

A **hairbrush** helps take the tangles out of your hair.

hairdryer

A hairdryer is a machine that dries your wet hair using hot air.

This **hairdryer** can dry wet hair in no time at all.

half

When you separate something into two equal parts, each part is one half of what you started with.

One **half** of this pizza looks as good as the other half!

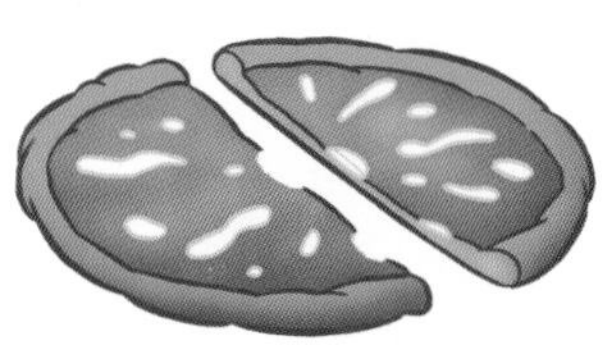

ham

Ham is a kind of meat that comes from a pig.

Ham and fresh vegetables makes a tasty dinner.

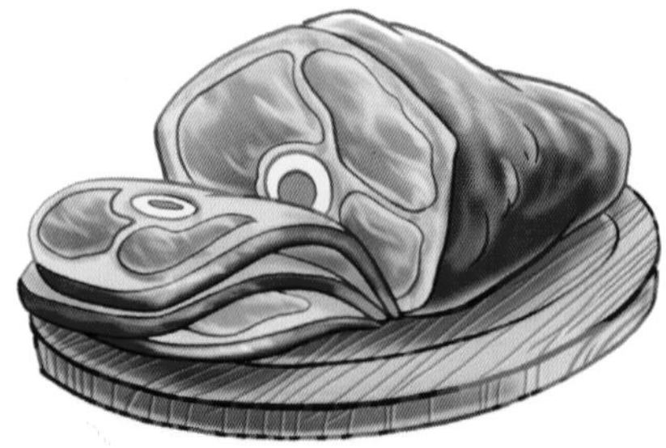

hamburger

A hamburger is made from minced meat, which is shaped into a flat circle and cooked.

What do you like in your **hamburger**?

hammock

A hammock is a swinging bed made of fabric or netting attached on either end to an upright object (usually a tree).

These Lost Boys are listening to a story in their **hammock**.

handle

A handle is something that you use to open a door or carry a bag.

Mickey turns the **handle** and opens the door.

happy

You are happy when you feel good about something.

Looking after Riley makes Joy **happy**!

hat

A hat is something you wear on your head.

This **hat** has such pretty decorations!

handsome

A man who has an attractive face is handsome.

Prince Phillip is **handsome** and kind.

hard

Something is hard when it doesn't bend or change shape easily.

Brrr! This floor is **hard** and cold.

hang

When you hang an object you attach it to something, so it dangles down.

Why would someone **hang** a toy in a tree?

harp

A harp is a large, heavy musical instrument that leans against you while you pluck the strings.

What wonderful **harp** music!

hate

When you hate something, you really don't like it at all.

Do you love or **hate** having broccoli for tea?

A B C D E F G H I J K L M N O P Q R S T U V W X Y Z

have

When you have something, it is with you at that moment, it is part of you or it belongs to you.

Are you allowed to **have** that apple, Goofy?

heavy

When something is heavy, it is difficult to lift.

Arlo is trapped under a **heavy** rock.

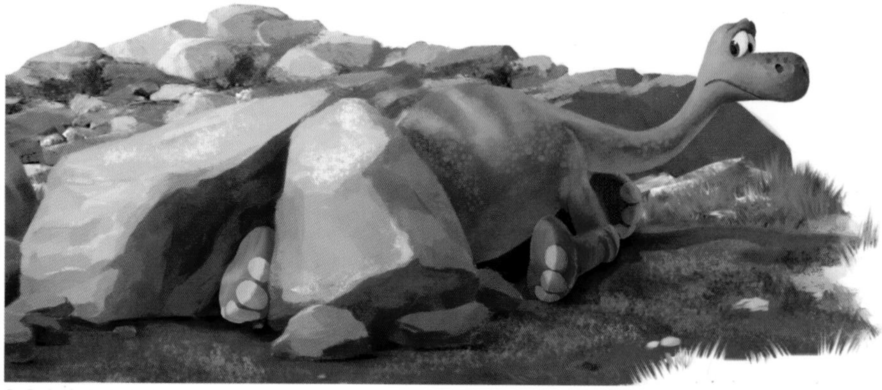

healthy

To be healthy means to feel well.

Sulley and Mike work hard to stay fit and **healthy**.

helicopter

A helicopter is a flying aircraft with blades on the top.

Blade Ranger is a fire and rescue **helicopter**.

help

When you help someone, you do something to make things easier for that person.

Elsa would do anything to **help** her little sister.

hear

When you hear something, it means you listen to the sounds that reach your ears.

Mr Stork can **hear** elephants on this train.

helmet

A helmet is a hard hat that protects your head from knocks and bumps.

Mickey always wears a **helmet** when he goes cycling.

here

Here means in this place.

Someone important sits **here**!

hide

To hide means to put something in a place where it cannot be found easily.

The puppies must **hide** under this bridge.

hippopotamus

A hippopotamus is an African animal with a large body and short legs that spends a lot of time in water.

A **hippopotamus** can move around more easily in water than on land.

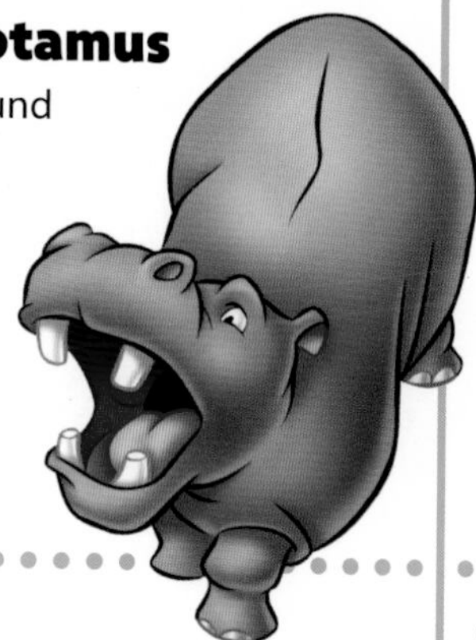

hold

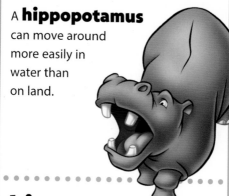

To hold something is to keep it in place.

Disgust wants to **hold** on to this memory ball.

high

Something that is high is far above something else.

Peter Pan and his friends soar **high** above Never Land.

hit

When you hit something, you strike it hard.

Wreck-It Ralph's fist can **hit** hard!

hole

A hole is a hollow space in something.

Rabbit lives in a **hole** in the ground.

hike

To hike is to take a long walk, often out in nature.

Kristoff and Sven have got a bit lost on their **hike**.

holiday

A holiday is when you take a trip away from home or school.

Olaf would like to go on a sunny **holiday**!

A B C D E F G H I J K L M N O P Q R S T U V W X Y Z

home

A home is the place where someone lives.

Home is a special place.

homework

Homework is schoolwork that you do at home.

Mike does his **homework** every single night.

hope

When you hope for something, you wish for it to happen.

Geppetto's greatest **hope** is to have a child of his own.

honey

Honey is a sticky, sweet syrup made by bees.

Abu has found a pot of golden **honey**.

horse

A horse is a large animal that neighs and has long legs, a long tail and hair on its neck called a mane.

When she goes onto the land, Ariel must learn to ride a **horse**.

hop

To hop is to jump.

Roo is a baby kangaroo who likes to **hop** up and down!

hospital

A hospital is a place where people go when they are sick and need special care to get better.

Doctors and nurses work in a **hospital**.

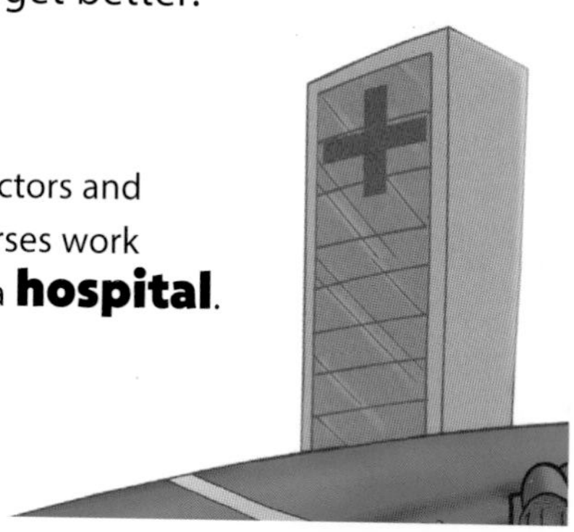

hot

Something hot is very warm.

It's good to take it easy on a **hot** day.

hotel

A hotel is a big building with lots of bedrooms, where people stay overnight when they are travelling.

This **hotel** has many floors.

hour

An hour is a period of time, made up of sixty minutes. There are twenty-four hours in a day.

Kanga's clock will ring in one **hour**.

house

A house is a building that people live in.

Riley and her family are moving to a new **house**.

hug

When you hug someone, you put your arms around them.

Baymax has big arms to **hug** with!

hungry

When you are hungry, you need something to eat.

Mickey and Minnie are feeling rather **hungry**.

hurry

When you hurry, you move fast because you want to get somewhere quickly.

When there's an emergency, it's time to **hurry**.

husband

A husband is a man who is married.

Tiana holds hands with her new **husband**.

Ii

ice

Ice is frozen water.

Ice can be very slippery indeed!

ice cream

Ice cream is a frozen dessert made of milk or cream and has sugar and flavourings such as chocolate or vanilla.

Mmm! It's easy to finish **ice cream** before it melts!

idea

An idea is a thought you have about something.

Joy has come up with the most wonderful **idea**.

ice skates

Ice skates are shoes with blades on the bottom. You wear them to skate on ice.

Kristoff wants to take off his **ice skates**, but Anna does not!

A B C D E F G H I J K L M N O P Q R S T U V W X Y Z

A B C D E F G H I J K L M N O P Q R S T U V W X Y Z

in

In means within or surrounded by.

Jafar did not know that the Genie lived **in** this lamp!

interesting

When something is interesting, you want to know more about it.

Belle thinks Beast's red rose is very **interesting**.

iron

An iron is a triangle-shaped device that smoothes out the wrinkles in clothes using heat and steam.

Don't touch the **iron**! It is hot.

Internet

The Internet is a worldwide network of computers that stores lots of information. When you want to find a website on your computer, you connect to the Internet.

The **Internet** can teach us about the world.

insect

An insect is an animal that usually has three pairs of legs and often two pairs of wings.

An ant is a common type of **insect**.

island

An island is a piece of land surrounded by water.

The Manta Jet flies Mr Incredible to a remote **island**.

Joy

Jj

jacket

A jacket is a kind of coat.

This **jacket** is a perfect fit!

jam

Jam is a sweet food made from fruit and sugar. You can spread it on bread.

What flavour **jam** do you like best?

jar

A jar is a glass container with a lid that holds food and other things.

This **jar** will keep your food fresh.

jeans

Jeans are trousers made with a type of cloth called denim.

Jeans are worn by people all over the world.

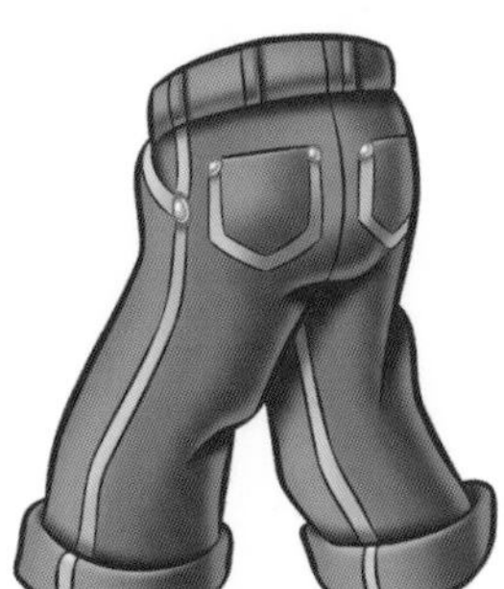

jewel

A jewel is a precious gemstone, such as a diamond.

Abu must take this **jewel** back to Aladdin!

jigsaw puzzle

A jigsaw puzzle is made up of pieces of a picture that have to be put together.

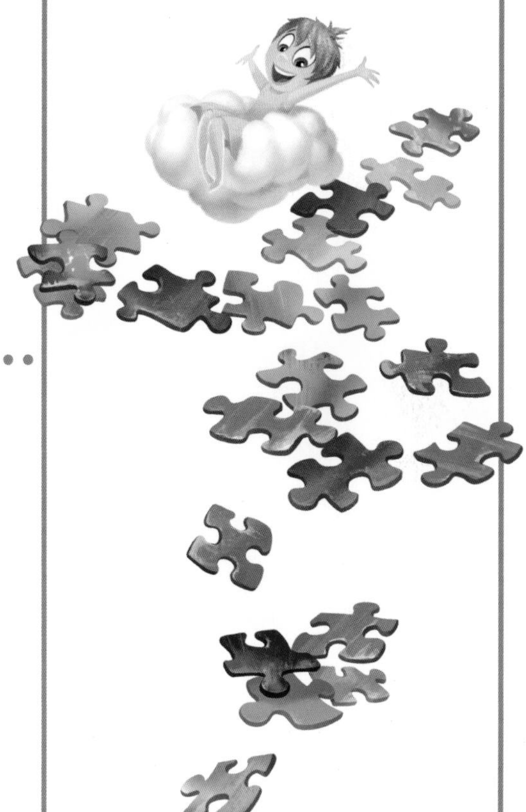

Joy's **jigsaw puzzle** has lots and lots of pieces.

joke

A joke is something that someone says to make you laugh.

Elsa's **joke** makes Anna giggle!

juice

Juice is the liquid you get when you squeeze fruit or vegetables.

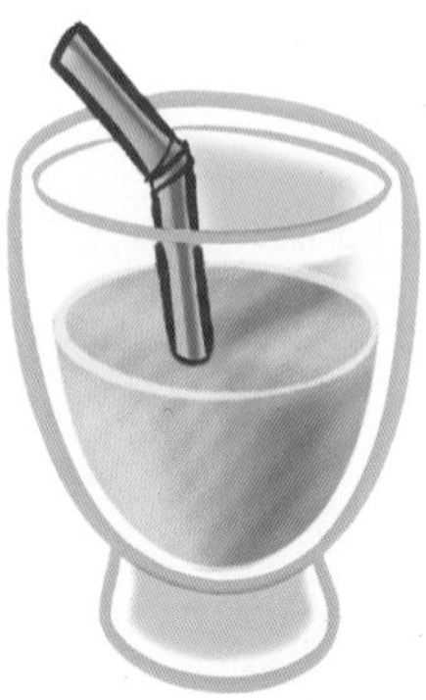

Apple **juice** is a drink made from squeezed apples.

jungle

A jungle is a warm place filled with trees, plants and wild animals.

Mowgli thinks that the **jungle** is the greatest place on Earth.

jump

When you jump, you push with both your feet off the ground and move up into the air.

Judy Hopps can **jump** over anything in her path!

Kristoff

Kk

kangaroo
A kangaroo is a jumping animal with big feet. The mother kangaroo carries her baby in a pouch in her belly.

Kanga is a brown **kangaroo** with a bouncy baby boy.

keep
When you keep something, you hold on to it.

Dumbo must use his trunk to **keep** this feather safe.

kennel
A kennel is a house for a dog, usually found in the garden.

Lady has her own **kennel** in the garden.

keyboard
A keyboard is a long row of buttons, either on a computer or a musical instrument.

Hiro types a message on his **keyboard**.

key
A key is a metal object that opens a lock.

King Fergus will not give up the **key** to his castle.

kick
When you kick, you deliver a strong, forceful motion with your foot or feet.

Baymax can **kick** harder than a human!

A B C D E F G H I J K L M N O P Q R S T U V W X Y Z

king

A king is a male ruler of a country.

Rapunzel takes the arm of her father, the **king**.

kitchen

A kitchen is the room where food is prepared and cleared away.

Donald is in his **kitchen** making a sandwich.

knife

A knife is a tool for cutting many things.

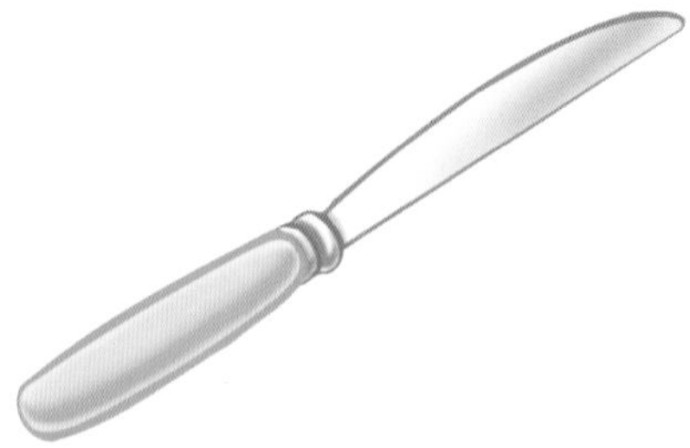

This **knife** is also good for spreading butter on bread.

kiss

A kiss is a touch you make with your lips.

Cinderella and Prince Charming share a special **kiss**.

kite

A kite is a toy on a string that flies in the wind.

Pooh's **kite** darts and dances in the wind.

knock

When you knock on something, you hit it with your closed fist to make a sound.

When Cruella visits, she doesn't even! bother to **knock**!

kitten

A kitten is a very young cat.

Marie is the cutest **kitten**.

know

When you know something, you have learned about it and remember it.

Do you **know** the name of Mulan's horse?

Lightning McQueen

Ll

lamp

A lamp gives off light and usually runs on electricity.

The **lamp** shines onto Hiro's desk.

last

The last one is the one that comes after all the others.

The **last** lemming wants a lolly, too!

laptop

A laptop is a computer that is small enough to carry around.

Riley uses her **laptop** to read about her friends back home.

ladder

A ladder is a long set of steps that you can move around and use to climb up high.

Belle climbs up to the top of the **ladder**.

large

Large is another word for big.

Angus is a **large** Shire horse.

late

Late means after the time something is supposed to happen.

Oh dear! The White Rabbit is going to be **late**!

A B C D E F G H I J K L M N O P Q R S T U V W X Y Z

laugh

When you laugh, you make a special sound that means you find something funny.

These dinosaurs like to sit and **laugh** around the campfire.

learn

To learn something means to gain knowledge.

These children have come to Tiana's class to **learn** about cooking!

leave

When you leave something, you go away from it.

Mulan must **leave** her village.

lazy

If you feel lazy, it means that you don't feel like doing anything.

Baloo is in the mood for a **lazy** day on the river.

left

Left is a position which is the opposite of right.

Ariel is floating to the **left** of Flounder.

leaf

A leaf is the flat part of a plant that grows on the stem or branch.

A **leaf** looks enormous to a tiny ant like Flik.

least

The least of something is the smallest part of it.

Broccoli is Disgust's **least** favourite vegetable.

lemon

A lemon is a yellow fruit that grows on a tree.

The juice from a **lemon** tastes sour on the tongue.

less

Less means not as much as something else.

Mike has **less** chance than Johnny of winning the Scare Games.

library

A library is a building with a lot of books you can borrow.

The **library** has many stories for you to take home to read!

lifeguard

A lifeguard is a person who works at a pool or beach to make sure people swim safely.

A **lifeguard** has to be a strong swimmer.

lesson

A lesson is something you learn that you didn't know before.

Hurry up, children! Mr Ray is starting his **lesson**.

lift (carry)

To lift something means to pick it up.

The mighty Genie can **lift** up a palace!

lettuce

Lettuce is a green vegetable with large leaves.

You must wash a **lettuce** before you put it in a salad.

lie

When people tell lies, they are saying something that is not true.

Every time Pinocchio tells a **lie**, his nose gets longer.

A B C D E F G H I J K L M N O P Q R S T U V W X Y Z

lift (device)

A lift is a little room or platform that goes up and down in a building, taking people from floor to floor.

You can take the **lift** all the way up to the top floor.

lightning

Lightning is the flash of light you see in the sky just before you hear thunder.

A bolt of **lightning** streaks towards the ground.

listen

When you listen to something or someone, you pay attention.

Anna agrees to **listen** to what Prince Hans has to say.

light (to see)

A light is a form of brightness.

Ray is an old firefly, but he still has a bright **light** on his body.

like

If you like something or someone, you feel good about them.

Do you **like** Lumière's new dance move?

litter

Litter is rubbish that needs to be recycled or thrown away.

WALL-E lives in a place that is piled high with **litter**.

light (to weigh)

If something is light, it doesn't weigh very much at all.

Gypsy the butterfly is as **light** as a feather.

lion

A lion is a large wild cat that roars. An adult male lion has a mane of fur around his neck.

Simba's father is a wise and good **lion** king.

live

To live means to be alive.

Pinocchio wants to **live** and breathe like a real boy.

living room
A living room is the room in a house where people spend a lot of time together.

The **living room** is the busiest part of the house!

look
When you look at something or someone, you pay attention to what you are seeing.

Ariel likes to **look** at treasures from the human world.

love
To love someone or something means you care a lot about them.

Anna and Elsa **love** each other very much.

long
When something is long, the beginning is far away from the end.

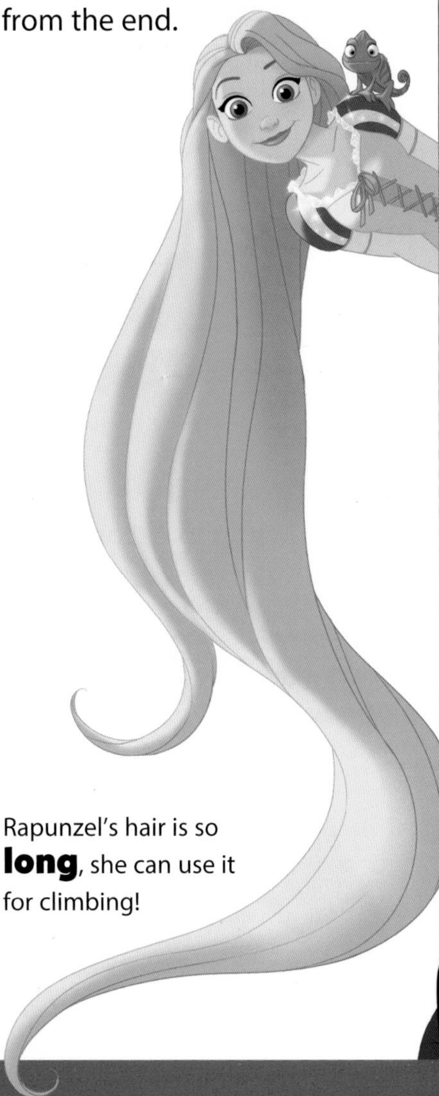

Rapunzel's hair is so **long**, she can use it for climbing!

lost
If you don't know where you are, you are lost.

Arlo is a **lost** and lonely dinosaur.

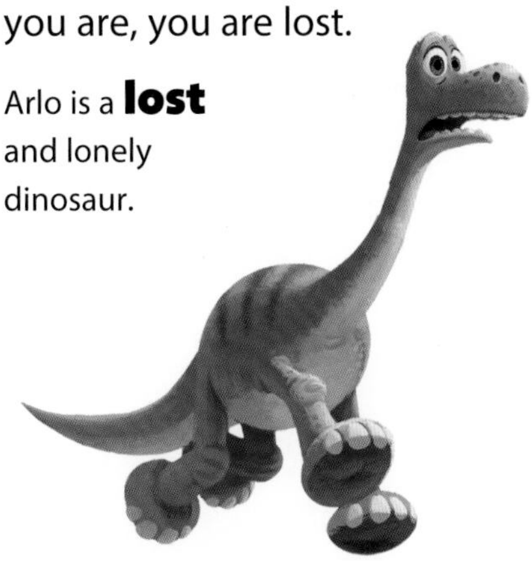

low
Something that is low is close to the ground.

Slinky Dog's tummy is wobbly and **low**.

loud
When something is loud, it is very noisy.

The Beast's roar is fierce and **loud**.

lunch
Lunch is the second meal of the day.

Mickey is having **lunch** by himself today.

A B C D E F G H I J K L M N O P Q R S T U V W X Y Z

Merida

Mm

machine

A machine is something built to do or make things.

Flik's new **machine** is ready to go!

magazine

A magazine is something that you can buy to read, which has lots of colour pictures, news and interesting information.

Do you collect a comic or a **magazine**?

magic

Magic is the power to make impossible things happen, using charms or spells.

A little **magic** turns Cinderella into a fairy-tale princess!

magnet

A magnet is a piece of iron or metal that can pull other pieces of metal towards it.

This **magnet** is very powerful.

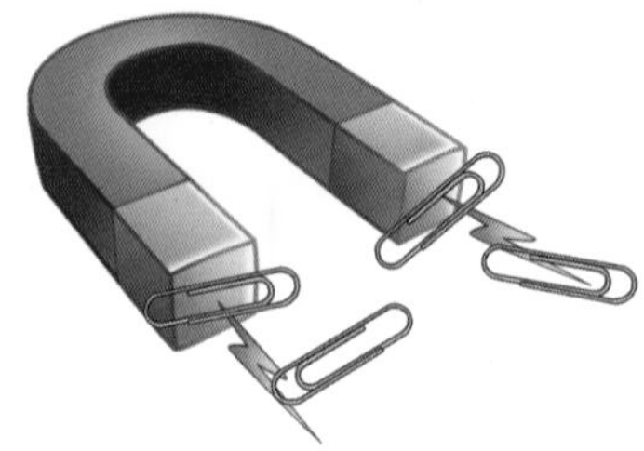

make

When you make something, you create it, put it together or change one thing into something else.

Flora and Merryweather are trying to **make** a dress for Aurora!

man

A boy grows up to become a man.

Mr Incredible is a **man** with superpowers.

map

A map is a picture that shows where places and locations are.

Queen Elinor can point to all the countries on this **map**.

match

When two things match, they are the same.

These otters are a perfect **match**!

maths

Maths is learning about numbers, counting and doing sums.

We all learn **maths** when we go to school.

me

Me is another way of referring to yourself, as well as 'I'.

This little bird says, "Look at **me**!"

meal

A meal is the food you eat at one time. You have three meals a day – breakfast, lunch and dinner.

Rapunzel eats every **meal** at the top of her tower.

mean

Someone who is mean is usually unkind.

Lucifer the cat can be sneaky and **mean**.

measure

When you measure something, you find out how tall, wide or deep it is.

The Genie is trying to **measure** Aladdin.

meat

Meat is part of an animal that is eaten as food.

This roasted **meat** is ready to serve.

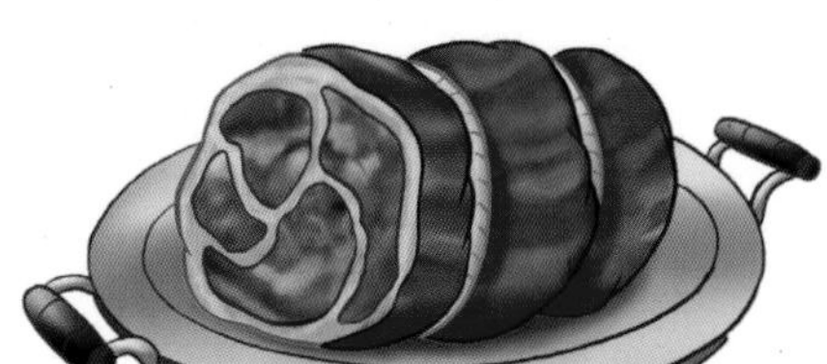

A B C D E F G H I J K L M N O P Q R S T U V W X Y Z

medicine

Medicine is something people take when they are unwell so that they can get better.

The doctor gives you **medicine** when you are poorly.

meet

When two people or things come together, they meet.

Prince Hans and Anna **meet** on the balcony.

melon

A melon is a big, ball-shaped fruit that is sweet and juicy inside.

A slice of fresh **melon** always tastes good!

melt

To melt means to go from being solid or frozen to being liquid.

Olaf will **melt** if he gets too close to the oven.

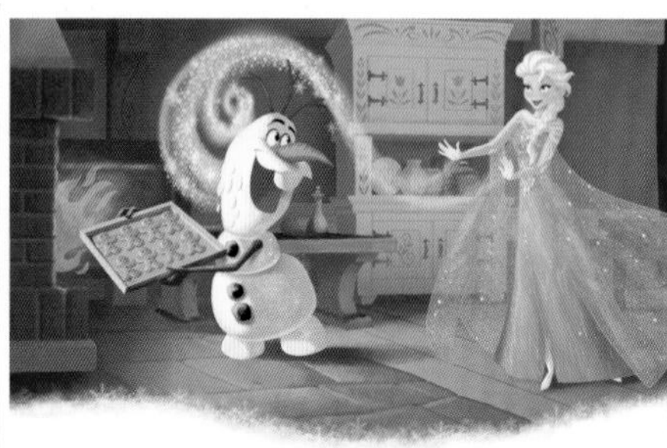

menu

A menu is a list of choices, usually of food.

There are so many delicious things on this **menu**.

mermaid

A mermaid is a girl or woman with human arms and a fishtail, who lives in the sea.

Ariel is a little **mermaid** with a green tail.

merry-go-round

A merry-go-round is a fairground ride where you sit on carved horses while the ride turns and plays music.

Do you like to ride on the **merry-go-round**?

microphone

A microphone is a machine that helps to record sounds or make sounds louder.

A **microphone** can be handy in a room full of people.

microwave

A microwave oven cooks food faster than a regular oven.

It looks like Donald Duck has been using this **microwave** oven!

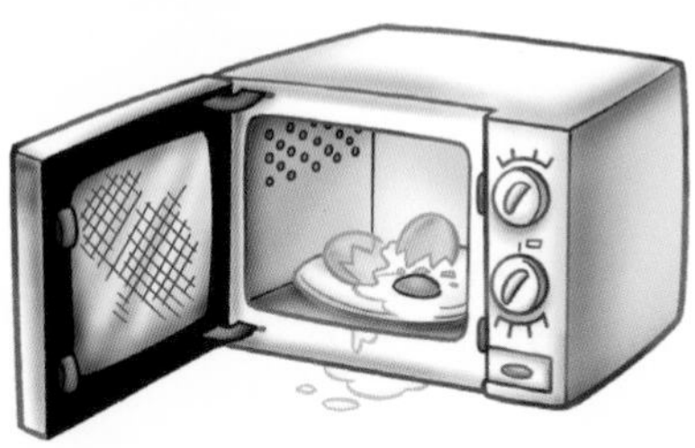

midday

Midday is the 12 o'clock hour during the day.

The afternoon starts a second after **midday**.

midnight

Midnight is 12 o'clock at night.

A new day starts a second after **midnight**.

milk

Milk is what you drink to make your bones strong.

This fresh **milk** comes from cows.

minute

A minute is made up of sixty seconds. There are sixty minutes in an hour.

Captain Hook's alarm clock will ring in one **minute**.

mirror

A mirror is a kind of glass in which you can see yourself.

When Ursula looks in the **mirror**, she sees her true reflection.

mistake

A mistake is when you do something wrong by accident.

Riley dropped her ice cream by **mistake**.

A B C D E F G H I J K L M N O P Q R S T U V W X Y Z

mix

When you mix things, you put them together to make something new.

Snow White will **mix** these ingredients together to make a pie!

monkey

A monkey is a furry animal with long legs and arms and usually a long tail.

Abu is the smartest **monkey** Aladdin has ever met.

moon

A moon is a round object that travels around a planet in space.

Tonight the **moon** is round and full.

mobile phone

A mobile phone is a phone you can carry and use anywhere.

Riley uses her **mobile phone** to message home.

monster

A monster is an imaginary creature that is often frightening and strange looking.

This **monster** has fluffy legs and no body!

money

Money is the coins and notes you use to pay for the things you want to buy.

The Coachman has brought a sack full of **money**.

month

A year is broken up into twelve months. A month usually has 30 or 31 days.

What is your birthday **month**?

morning

Morning is the early part of the day, before noon.

Mickey and Pluto get up early every **morning**.

most
Most means the largest part of something.

Pooh has eaten **most** of his honey.

mouse (animal)
A mouse is a small grey or brown animal with long whiskers and a long tail. A mouse says, "Squeak! Squeak!"

Gus is a small **mouse** with a big appetite!

museum
A museum is a building that contains interesting things for you to look at and learn about.

What is your favourite **museum**?

mountain
A mountain is a very large, steep hill.

Sometimes a **mountain** has snow at the top.

mouse (computer)
A mouse is a device you move around and click to make things happen on your computer.

Move the **mouse** to make the computer work.

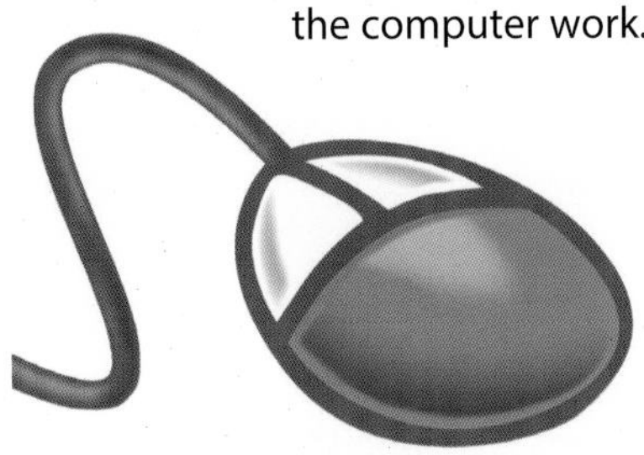

mushroom
A mushroom is a fungus that grows in dark, damp places.

Only some types of **mushroom** are safe to eat.

moustache
A moustache is hair that a man grows between his nose and lips.

This mind worker is proud of his neat **moustache**.

music
Music is a tune made by singing or playing a musical instrument.

Music sounds sweeter if you share it with others.

A B C D E F G H I J K L M N O P Q R S T U V W X Y Z

A B C D E F G H I J K L M N O P Q R S T U V W X Y Z

Nn

napkin
A napkin is a square piece of cloth or paper that you use to wipe your hands and face while you eat.

This **napkin** would be perfect for a smart dinner party!

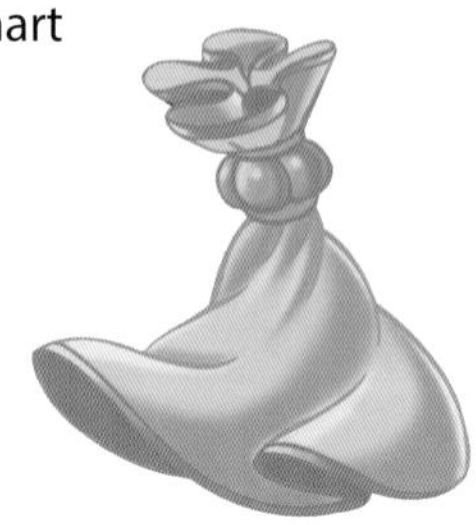

neighbour
A neighbour is someone who lives very close to you.

Mickey's new **neighbour** is Minnie Mouse.

near
Something that is near is close by.

The planes are flying **near** to the Statue of Liberty.

nail
Nails are thin pieces of metal, with a point at one end, that are hammered into wood to hold things together.

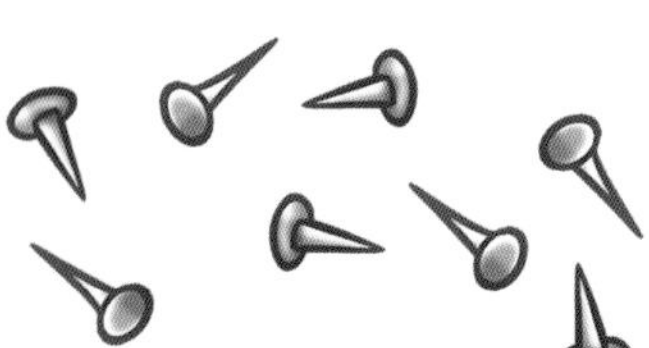

A **nail** can hold up a picture or even help make a shelf.

need
When you need something, you cannot do without it.

Olaf will **need** to stay cold at all times otherwise he will melt.

nephew
Your nephew is the male child of your sister or brother.

Cass is very proud of her clever **nephew**.

nest
A nest is a place where birds lay eggs. A nest can also be a home to mice, squirrels or other small animals.

This bird is delivering breakfast to her chicks in their **nest**.

new
When something is new, it means that it has just been made or has never been used.

The Incredibles have smart, **new** Super Hero costumes.

nice
If someone or something is nice, it means you like them.

Ariel thinks Flounder is a very **nice** friend.

netball
This is a sports game where players have to work as a team to get a ball into a high net.

This is the ball and net used in a **netball** match.

newspaper
A newspaper has all the daily news printed on big sheets of folded paper.

Have you looked at a **newspaper** today?

niece
A niece is the female child of your sister or brother.

Mickey's **niece** has got a new trick!

never
Never means not ever or at no time.

Sven will **never** leave his friend, Kristoff.

next
If you are next to someone, you are right beside them.

Lightning and Sally have parked up **next** to each other.

night

Night is the time between evening and morning when the sky is dark.

The **night** is cool and filled with stars.

north

North is the opposite direction of south. North is at the top of a map.

The pointer for **north** is at the top of the compass.

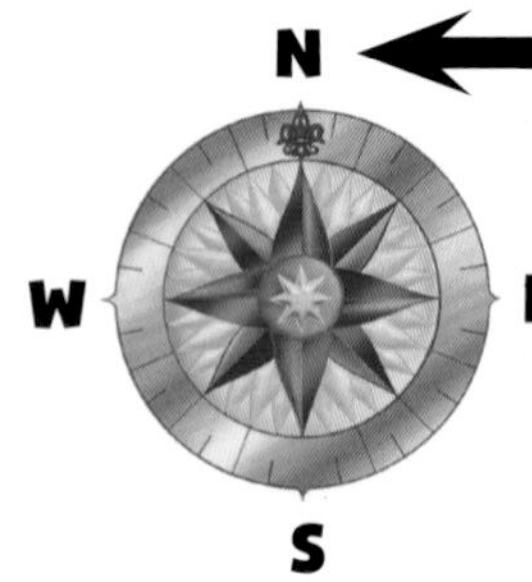

no

When someone says no, that means they don't believe something, don't want to do something or disagree with something.

Anger says "**No** way!"

no one

No one means not anyone at all.

Wreck-It Ralph has **no one** to play with.

notebook

A notebook is a book with blank pages that you use for writing things down.

You could write a poem or a story in this **notebook**.

noise

A noise is a sound made by someone or something.

All of Donald's hammering was making a lot of **noise**!

nothing

Nothing means not anything at all.

Jasmine is certain that this lamp has **nothing** inside it.

now

Now means at this time.

Now Rapunzel and her family are together again.

nurse

A nurse is someone who cares for you if you are hurt or poorly.

Baymax is a **nurse** robot.

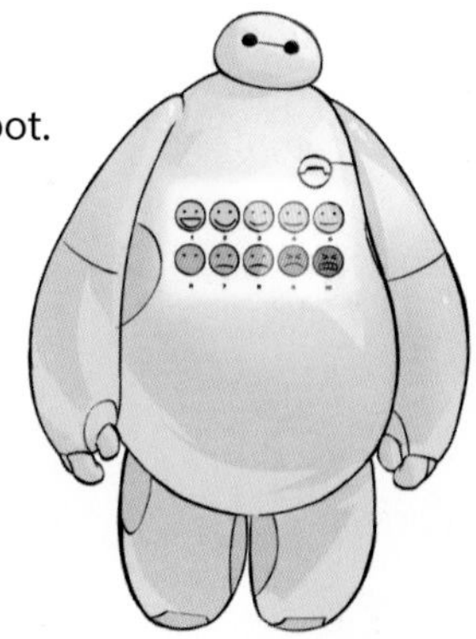

nut

A nut is a small fruit with a hard shell.

Sometimes you must crack a **nut** before you can eat it.

numbers

Numbers are units used for counting and for doing sums.

Can you count the **numbers** from one to ten?

1 one
2 two
3 three
4 four
5 five
6 six
7 seven
8 eight
9 nine
10 ten

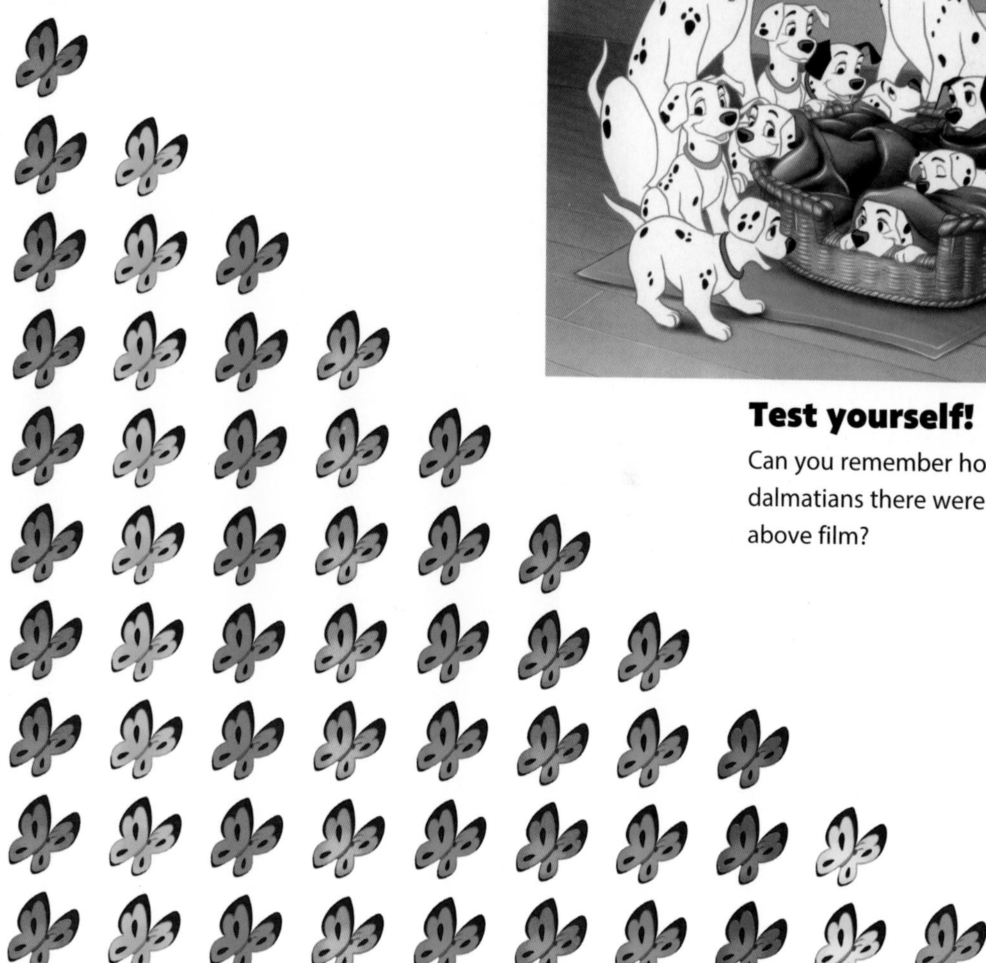

Test yourself!

Can you remember how many dalmatians there were in the above film?

A B C D E F G H I J K L M N O P Q R S T U V W X Y Z

Oo

octopus

An octopus is an animal with eight long arms that lives in the sea.

Hank is an unusual **octopus** – he only has seven arms.

office

An office is a place with desks and computers where people go to work.

Bob Parr works in an **office** every day.

old

Something or someone old has been around for a long time.

Stinky Pete is a very **old** cowboy toy.

omelette

An omelette is made of beaten eggs that are fried in a pan.

Do you like cheese in your **omelette**?

on

When someone is on something, he or she is over and supported by the object underneath.

Olaf the snowman is riding **on** Sven's back!

onion

An onion is a round vegetable that grows underground with a strong taste and smell.

Chopping an **onion** can bring tears to your eyes!

ostrich

The ostrich is one of the few birds that does not fly, but it can run very fast.

An **ostrich** is the largest bird in the world.

oven

An oven is something you have in your kitchen that heats up and cooks food.

There's a freshly baked pie inside this **oven**!

open

When something is closed, you open it to get inside.

Open the paintbox and see what you can find.

over

Over means above or on top of. It can also mean finished.

Arlo and Spot gaze **over** the clouds.

orange

An orange is a round, orange-coloured fruit with thick skin and a sweet taste.

Squeeze an **orange** and you will get sweet juice!

out

When something is out, it has been removed from the place it was.

Joy and her friends tumble **out** of the train.

owl

An owl is a bird with large round eyes. It says "twit twoo!"

An **owl** prefers to sleep during the day.

A B C D E F G H I J K L M N O P Q R S T U V W X Y Z

Pocahontas

Pp

paint

When you paint something, such as a picture or a wall, you cover it with a coloured liquid, using a paintbrush.

There is **paint** all over the floor!

painter

A painter is someone who paints.

Rapunzel is a keen **painter**.

palace

A palace is a big and beautiful home for royalty, such as a king, queen, prince or princess.

This **palace** has towers and turrets.

page

A page is one sheet of printed paper within a book, magazine or newspaper.

There is a picture of a princess on this **page**.

pair

A pair means two of a kind.

This **pair** of horseshoes will help a horse trot!

pan

A pan is a container used for cooking.

The potatoes are bubbling in the **pan**.

panda

A panda is a large animal with black-and-white fur. It is a type of bear.

This **panda** has never seen anyone quite like Goofy!

parents

Parents are the mothers and fathers of children.

Judy Hopps' **parents** are pleased when their daughter comes to visit.

panther

A panther is a large, wild member of the cat family.

Bagheera is the **panther** that first found Mowgli.

parade

A parade is a group of people, including musicians, marching together down a street to celebrate something.

The **parade** is making its way into the castle.

paper

Paper is a thin material made from ground-up wood. It is used for printing, writing, drawing, wrapping packages and many other things.

This old scroll is an ancient type of **paper**!

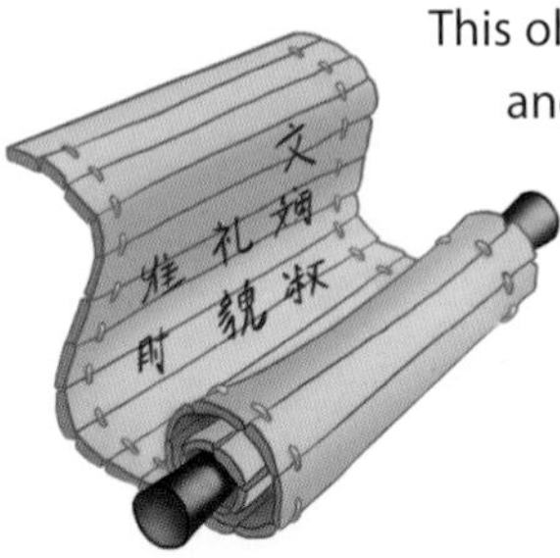

parcel

A parcel is a package that is wrapped up in paper.

Uncle Scrooge wrapped up every **parcel** in this sack!

park

A park is the grassy place where you go to enjoy being outside.

This **park** has lots of winding pathways.

A B C D E F G H I J K L M N O P Q R S T U V W X Y Z

parrot

A parrot is a bird with a hooked beak and bright feathers. Some parrots can talk.

Iago is Jafar's sly and scheming **parrot**.

pay

When you pay for something, you give somebody money in exchange for it.

Flynn agrees to **pay** two gold coins for some vegetables.

passengers

A passenger is someone riding on a form of transport.

There are two **passengers** riding on this tram.

pavement

A pavement is a cement path next to a road, for people to walk along.

People walk along the **pavement** with their dogs.

peach

A peach is a round fruit with yellow and red skin that grows on a peach tree.

A **peach** tastes so refreshing on a hot summer's day!

pasta

Pasta is a boiled food made of flour and water, often eaten with a sauce.

Mickey has made a plate of tomato **pasta**.

paw

A paw is the hand or foot of some animals.

A rabbit's **paw** is soft and fluffy.

pear

A pear is a bell-shaped fruit that grows on a pear tree.

When a **pear** is soft to touch, it is ready to eat.

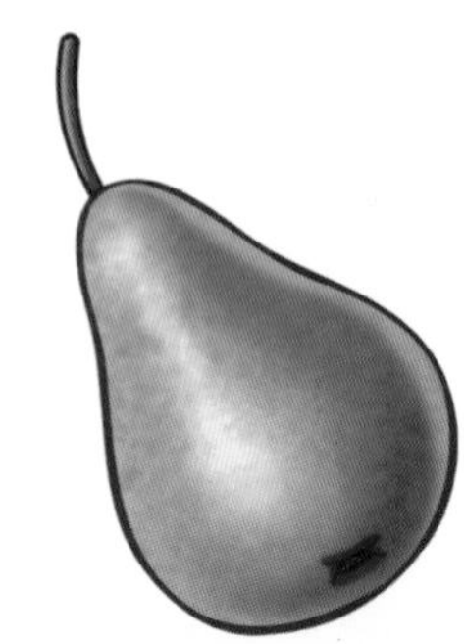

peas
Peas are small, round, green vegetables that grow in little containers called pods.

Peatey, Peatrice and Peanelope are three **peas** in a pod!

penguin
Penguins are black and white birds. Most live in very cold places.

A **penguin** cannot fly, but it is very good at waddling.

pepper (spice)
Pepper is a spice you use to flavour food. It is often used together with salt.

If you breathe it in, **pepper** can make you sneeze. Atishoo!

pen
A pen is something filled with ink and used for writing and drawing.

Tiana uses a **pen** to make a list.

people
People are men, women and children.

This group of **people** are heading off to San Fransokyo.

pencil
A pencil has a coloured or grey centre and is used for writing and drawing.

Elsa holds a **pencil** in her hand.

pepper (fruit)
A pepper is a fruit that can have a mild or very hot taste and comes in many colours.

A red **pepper** tastes a little sweeter than a green **pepper**.

pet
A pet is an animal that lives with you and that you take care of.

Prince Eric's **pet** dog Max has a very waggy tail.

photograph

A photograph is a picture that you take by using a camera.

Every time he takes a special **photograph**, Carl puts it in a frame.

picnic

A picnic is a meal you have outdoors, often sitting on a blanket which is spread on the ground.

When the sun is shining, it's a good day to have a **picnic**.

photographer

A photographer is someone who takes photographs.

Mike must sit still for the **photographer**.

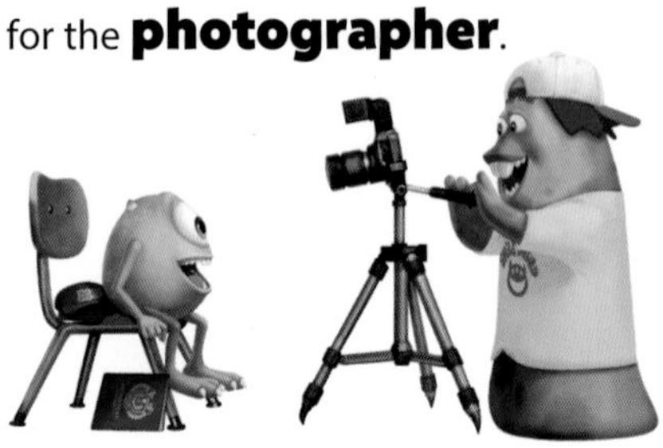

picture

You can make a picture by painting, drawing or photographing something or someone.

Rapunzel has painted a **picture** of Maximus.

pig

A pig is an animal with a fat body, short legs and curly tail. It says, "Oink, oink!"

Pua is Moana's playful pet **pig**.

piano

A piano is a large musical instrument with eighty-eight black and white keys.

You can use two hands and even your feet to play the **piano**.

pie

A pie is a round, baked food with a crust and a filling.

There are all sorts of yummy **pie** fillings. Which do you like best?

pillow

A pillow is a rectangular cloth sack filled with something soft, such as feathers, that you rest your head on while you sleep.

A soft, puffy **pillow** can help you drift off to sleep.

pilot
A pilot is someone who flies an aircraft or flying machine.

Abigail Callaghan is a skilful **pilot**.

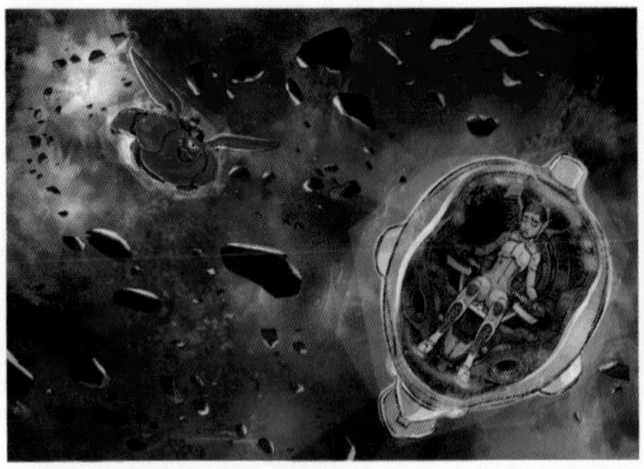

planet
A planet is a huge ball of rock or gas that travels around the Sun. Our Earth is a planet.

From the Moon, our **planet** looks like a round ball.

pineapple
A pineapple is a large fruit with a thick skin and leaves, which grows in hot places.

There is sweet, juicy fruit underneath the tough skin of this **pineapple**.

plant
A plant is any living thing that is not an animal.

A **plant** needs light and water to help it grow.

play (show)
A play is a story that is acted out on a stage in front of an audience.

When she was little, Judy starred in the school **play**!

pirate
A pirate is someone who travels the seas to find ships to rob.

Hook is a cruel and cunning **pirate** captain.

plate
A plate is a round, flat dish that can be used to serve food.

This **plate** goes on the dinner table.

play (engage in)
To play means to do activities just for the fun of it.

Elsa and Anna love to **play** in the snow.

playground

A playground is an outdoor place with swings, slides and seesaws where you go to play.

The new **playground** is ready for visitors!

plum

A plum is a fruit that grows on a plum tree.

A **plum** must be ripe before you can eat it.

pocket

A pocket is a small cloth bag sewn into your clothing, used to carry small things.

Don keeps his business cards in his top **pocket**.

police officer

A police officer protects people from crime.

Judy Hopps is proud to be a Zootropolis **police officer**.

police station

A police station is where you go to report a crime.

Judy meets Bellwether at the **police station**.

pollution

Pollution is something that is harmful to the environment.

Pollution can be in the air, on land or in the sea.

pond

A pond is a small area of water in a garden or a park.

Frogs, fish and ducks like to live in a **pond**.

poor

When someone is poor, it means that he or she has very little or no money.

Tramp is a **poor** dog, but he is very happy.

popcorn
Popcorn is a snack food made from a kind of corn that puffs up when heated.

Popcorn can be sprinkled with salt or sugar, or it can be coated in toffee.

post office
A post office is where people go to send letters and other mail and to buy postage stamps.

The **post office** will be open very soon.

pour
When you pour something, you make a liquid flow in a steady stream.

Fa Zhou asks Mulan to **pour** him a cup of tea.

postcard
When you are on holiday, you can use a postcard to send a message to your family and friends.

It's fun to receive a **postcard** in the post!

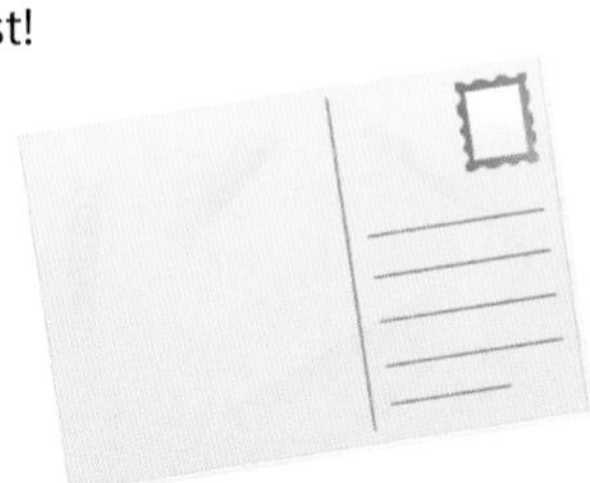

pot
A pot is a deep container used for cooking.

Look at all the food in the **pot**!

poster
A poster is a piece of paper that you hang on a wall. It has pictures or information on it.

Flynn Rider recognises the face on this **poster**!

potato
A potato is a vegetable that grows underground.

A **potato** tastes good boiled, baked, mashed or fried.

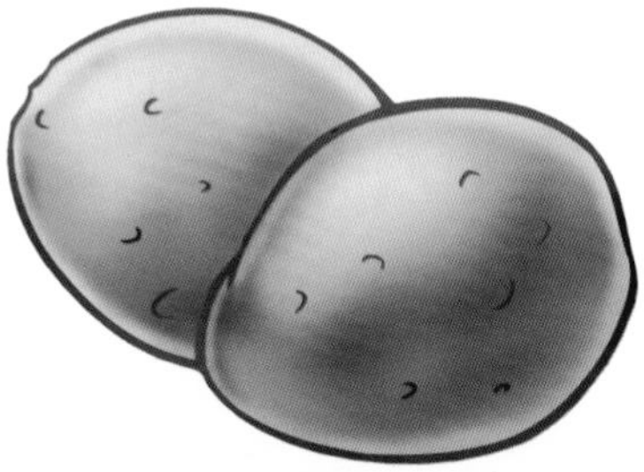

present
A present is a gift you give to someone.

Jock has been given a smart coat as a Christmas **present**.

A B C D E F G H I J K L M N O P Q R S T U V W X Y Z

price

The price of something is the amount of money it costs to buy it.

What is the **price** of this bow?

princess

A princess is the daughter of a sultan, king or queen.

Princess Jasmine is looking for a new adventure.

prince

A prince is the son of a sultan, king or queen.

Hans is the thirteenth **prince** from the Southern Isles.

printer

A printer is a machine attached to your computer that prints out on paper what you see on the screen.

This **printer** can print in colour and black and white.

pudding

A pudding is a cooked, sweet food, usually eaten after lunch or dinner.

Which **pudding** do you like the best?

problem

A problem is a difficult thing that you have to figure out how to solve.

Uh-oh. The bugs have a big, bird-shaped **problem!**

pull

When you pull something, you tug it towards you.

Mickey uses a trolley to **pull** the picnic things.

pumpkin

A pumpkin is a large, round, orange fruit that grows on a vine.

A **pumpkin** with a candle inside means that it's Halloween.

puppy

A puppy is a very young dog.

Pongo would do anything to save a **puppy** in trouble.

put

To put means to place something somewhere.

Judy has **put** a parking ticket on this car.

puppet

A puppet is a kind of doll that appears to move. There are hand puppets and puppets with strings.

This **puppet** can only move when the strings are pulled.

purse

A purse is a small leather or fabric pouch in which people keep their money and bank cards.

Ariel puts treasures in her **purse**.

push

When you push something, you press it with your hand to move it.

Buzz must **push** the toy back into its box.

pyjamas

Pyjamas are clothes that you sleep in at night.

Comfy **pyjamas** make you feel snuggly and warm.

A B C D E F G H I J K L M N O P Q R S T U V W X Y Z

Queen of Hearts

Qq

queen
A queen is a female ruler of a country.

Alice curtsies before the **Queen** of Hearts.

question
A question is something you ask when you need some information. When you ask a question, you want an answer.

Mother Gothel has a **question** for Rapunzel.

queue
A queue is a line of people or vehicles, all waiting for the same thing.

Nick and Judy haven't got time for this **queue**!

quick
Quick is another word for fast.

Pocahontas is a **quick** and nimble runner.

quiet
When something is quiet, there is little or no sound.

The Incredibles' household is about to go **quiet** as everyone goes to sleep.

quilt
A quilt is a cover for a bed. It has a soft filling inside, like goose feathers.

Hiro pushes back his **quilt** when he gets out of bed.

quiz
A quiz is a question and answer game where you are tested on what you know.

Do you know the answers to the **quiz** questions?

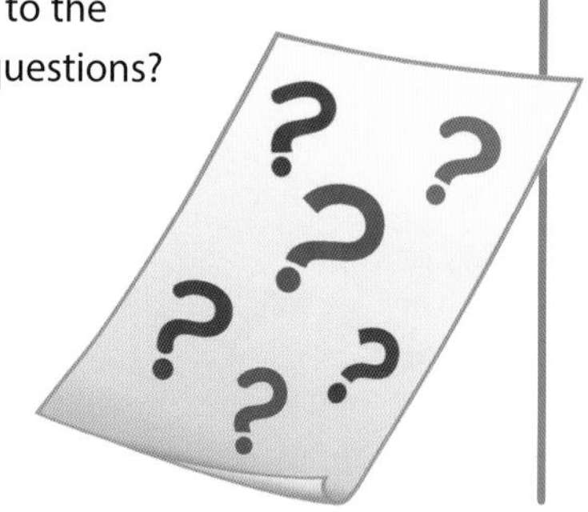

Rapunzel

Rr

rabbit
A rabbit is an animal with soft fur, long ears, big feet and a round, short tail.

Judy Hopps is a hard-working **rabbit**.

race
A race is a contest to see who is the fastest.

The **race** is on between Lightning McQueen and Chick Hicks!

radio
A radio is something that picks up broadcasts from radio stations so you can listen to what they are saying and the music they are playing.

Let's turn on the **radio**!

rain
Rain is drops of water that fall from clouds.

The **rain** pours down on Arlo and Spot.

rainbow
A rainbow is the wide band of colours that sometimes stretches across the sky after it rains.

Bing Bong's wagon rocket leaves a **rainbow** trail behind it.

reach
When you reach for something, you stretch your hand out towards it.

Aladdin tries to **reach** up and grab the old man's hand.

read

When you read, you look at words and understand what they mean.

Mike has got a stack of books to **read**.

referee

A referee is someone who makes sure that the rules of a game are followed.

Goofy is a very strict football **referee**!

remember

When you remember something or someone, you have not forgotten that person or thing.

Dory can't **remember** where her family lives.

receipt

A receipt is a piece of paper that tells what you have bought and how much it cost.

Daisy Duck has a large **receipt** from her last shopping trip!

refrigerator

A refrigerator is a machine that keeps food cold and fresh.

Minnie Mouse takes a look inside the **refrigerator**.

recycle

When you recycle an object, it can be used again. Bottles, cans and paper can all be recycled.

It's WALL-E's job to **recycle** the rubbish that he finds on Earth.

relative

A relative is someone in your family.

Every **relative** in Riley's family loves ice hockey!

remote control

A remote control lets you operate something, such as a television set or a toy car, from a distance.

Hiro uses a **remote control** to guide the robot.

repair

You repair or fix something that is broken.

The old man knows how to **repair** broken toys.

reporter

A reporter is a person who gathers news for a newspaper, magazine or radio or television station.

Mr Incredible gives an interview to the **reporter**.

restaurant

A restaurant is where people go to eat and pay for their meals.

Lady and Tramp are eating at their favourite **restaurant**.

A B C D E F G H I J K L M N O P Q R S T U V W X Y Z

rhinoceros
A rhinoceros is a large animal with thick skin and one or two horns on its nose.

The **rhinoceros** is found in Africa and Asia.

rich
Someone who is rich has a lot of money.

Aladdin could get used to being a **rich** man!

right (direction)
Right is the opposite direction of left.

Mrs Potts is standing to the **right** of Chip.

Left → Right

ribbon
A ribbon is a long, thin colourful strip of material used to tie something together.

Tinker Bell tugs on the **ribbon** as hard as she can.

ride
When you ride in or on something, you move along with it.

Tadashi and Hiro **ride** through the city.

right (correct)
Right is also the opposite of wrong. If you do something the right way, you do it correctly.

Merida shoots her arrows at the target, until she gets it **right**.

rice
Rice is a grain that is grown in warm, wet places.

Can you use chopsticks to eat **rice**?

ridge
A ridge is a long, narrow raised part of a surface, especially a high edge along a mountain.

Simba watches his father from a **ridge** as he runs away.

river
A river is a large stream of flowing water that moves from a high place, such as a mountain, to a lower place, such as the sea.

A **river** runs through this valley.

road

A road is a solid track that cars, bikes and other vehicles can travel along.

This **road** leads into the city.

rock

A rock is a very hard piece of the Earth. There are lots of different kinds of rock.

Rafiki stands on a tall **rock**, so that everyone can see Simba.

rocket

A rocket is a powerful machine that can blast into space.

Baymax has a **rocket** on his fist.

roll

When something rolls, it moves by turning over and over.

Pluto loves to **roll** in fresh grass!

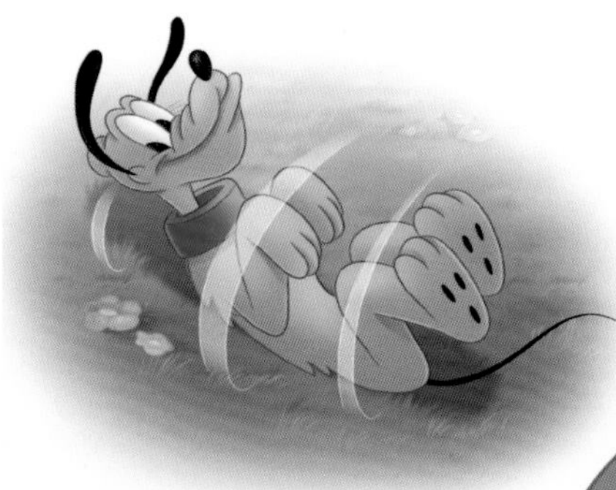

rope

Rope is a strong, thick string.

Oh no! Marshmallow has let go of the **rope**!

ruler

A ruler is a long, flat piece of wood, metal or plastic that helps you measure the length of something.

A **ruler** can help you draw straight lines.

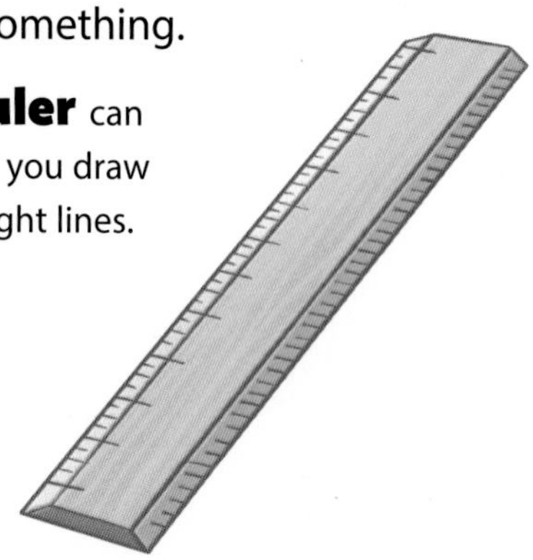

run

When you run, you move quickly, using your legs.

Mulan can **run** faster than anyone in her village.

A B C D E F G H I J K L M N O P Q R S T U V W X Y Z

Simba

Ss

sad
When a person is unhappy about something, he or she feels very sad.

Everybody feels **sad** from time to time.

saddle
A saddle is what you sit on when you ride a horse.

Maximus will only let Rapunzel put his **saddle** on him.

sail
When you sail, you ride on a boat that has sails.

Moana and Maui **sail** across the ocean.

salad
A salad is a mixture of leaves, such as lettuce, vegetables and fruit that you eat cold.

Mickey uses spoons to mix up the **salad**.

salt
Salt comes out of the ground or the sea and is added to food as a seasoning.

The **salt** is kept in the kitchen.

same
When two things are the same, it means they are alike.

These little bluebirds all look the **same**.

sand

Sand is made of tiny pieces of rock and is found along the beach, under the sea and in the desert.

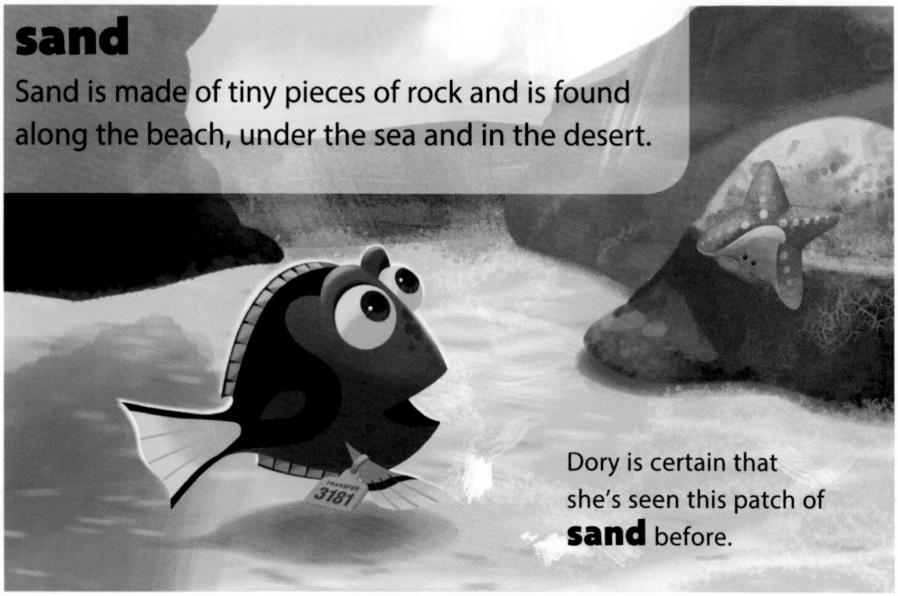

Dory is certain that she's seen this patch of **sand** before.

saucer

A saucer is a small dish, made to hold a teacup.

Fauna prefers to drink her tea from a teacup and **saucer**.

sandals

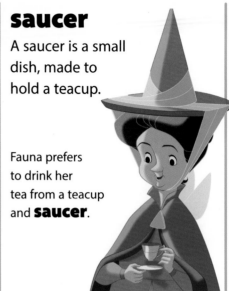

Sandals are shoes with lots of open spaces to keep your feet cool in warm weather.

When you wear **sandals**, everyone can see your toes!

sandpit

A sandpit is a big outdoor box, filled with sand.

You can dig for hours in a **sandpit**.

sausage

A sausage is a mixture of meat and spices, rolled up together.

A **sausage** tastes good grilled, baked or fried.

sandcastle

A sandcastle is a building you make out of sand.

Elsa and Anna have built a very fine **sandcastle**.

sandwich

A sandwich is two pieces of bread with some kind of filling in the middle.

What kind of **sandwich** do you like to eat?

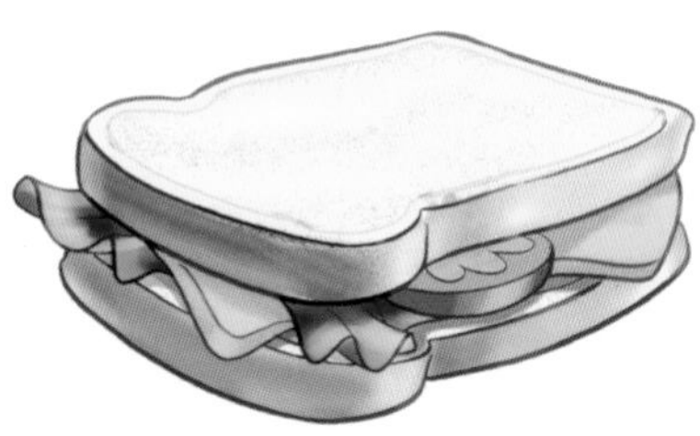

save

When you save something, you keep it because you want to have it later.

Randall has decided to **save** these cupcakes for Mike.

saw
A saw is a long metal tool with many sharp teeth used to cut pieces of wood.

A **saw** can be used to cut down trees or cut up logs.

saxophone
A saxophone is a musical instrument shaped a little like the letter S.

This **saxophone** is very shiny indeed.

scarf
A scarf is a long piece of cloth, usually wool, that you wrap around your neck to keep warm.

When it's cold outside, you need to wear a **scarf**.

scary
When something is scary, a person is afraid of it.

Could that be a **scary** monster or is this just a bad dream?

school
School is where you go to learn many exciting new things.

Moana goes to the island **school**.

scientist
A scientist is a person who tries to find things out by doing experiments.

Honey Lemon is studying to be a **scientist**.

scissors
A pair of scissors is a tool that people use to cut things.

You can use safety **scissors** to cut shapes out of paper.

scratch
You scratch an itch by rubbing it with something sharp, such as your fingernails.

Spot likes to **scratch** his ear with his big toe!

scream

When you scream, you make a very loud high-pitched sound with your voice, without using words.

Terri and Terry can **scream** twice as loud as other monsters!

screen

The screen of your TV or computer is the glass part at the front.

Everyone gathers around the **screen**.

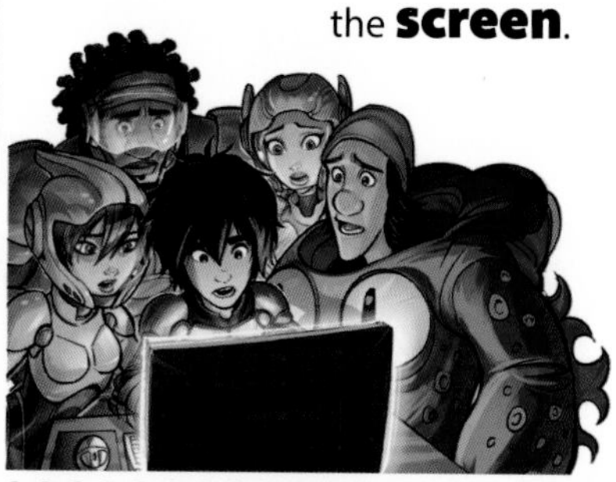

sea

The sea is a large area of salt water.

Ariel lives in the **sea**.

seagull

A seagull is a large, white bird that lives near the sea, where it feeds on fish.

Every **seagull** in the bay is looking down at Dory and Nemo.

screwdriver

A screwdriver is a tool that pushes screws into wood.

Hold the **screwdriver** by the handle, then turn it slowly.

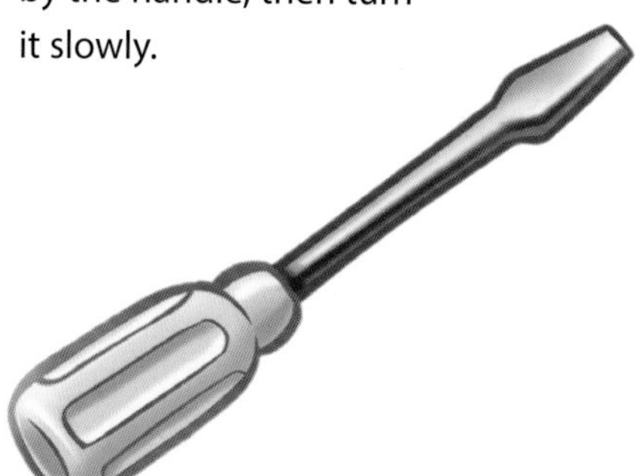

seafood

Seafood includes all of the animals that live in water that people can eat.

Some people like to order **seafood** when they go to a restaurant.

sea lion

A sea lion is an animal that lives in and around the sea and uses flippers to move around.

This **sea lion** has brown fur and flappy flippers.

seasons

Seasons are the four different parts of the year called spring, summer, autumn and winter.

The **seasons** change every few months.

second

There are sixty seconds in one minute.

This pocket watch ticks once every **second**.

secret

A secret is something you don't want everyone to know.

Merida and Queen Elinor share a **secret**.

see

When you look at something with your eyes, you can see it.

The dinosaurs **see** a strange light in the sky.

seed
A seed is the part of a fruit or flower that can grow into another plant.

Plant a **seed** and watch it grow!

sentence
A sentence is a set of words that make sense together.

Princess Atta doesn't want to hear Flik's **sentence**.

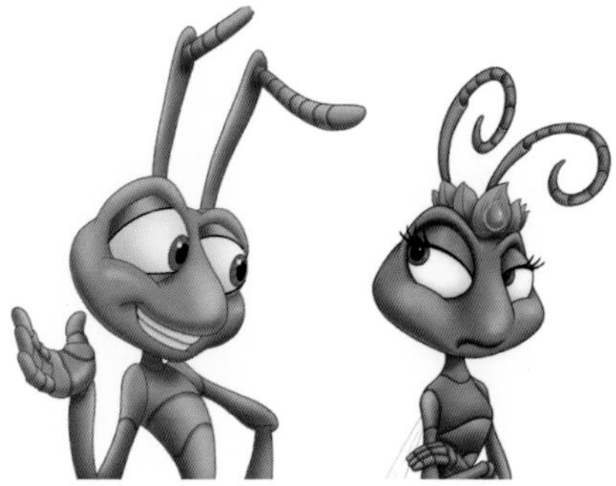

shake
To give something a shake means that you move it up and down or side to side very quickly.

Sebastian likes to shimmy and **shake** to the music.

sell
If you decide to sell something, you let someone else have it for money.

Nick wants to **sell** as many lollies as he can.

sew
When someone sews, they join pieces of cloth together, using a needle and thread.

The mice want to **sew** a gown for Cinderella.

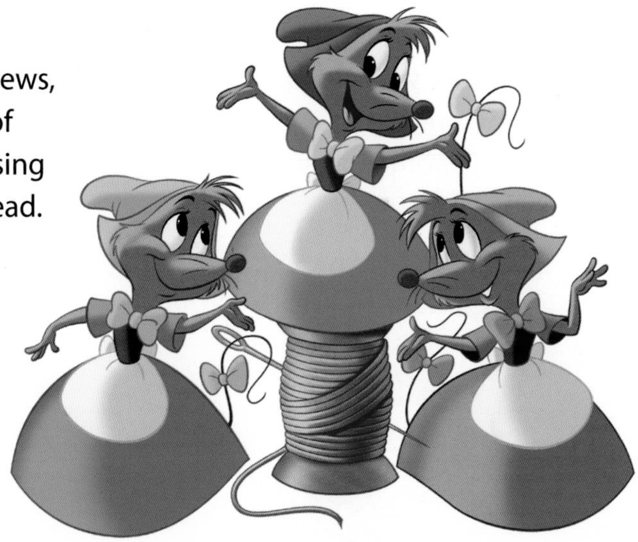

send
When you send something, you make it go from one place to another.

Lady decides to **send** Tramp away.

shadow
When you stand in the sun, the dark shape your body makes on the ground is called your shadow.

Simba's **shadow** follows him everywhere!

shampoo
Shampoo is liquid soap you use to wash your hair.

Shampoo has a nice, clean smell.

A B C D E F G H I J K L M N O P Q R S T U V W X Y Z

shapes

If you draw around the outside of something, you will draw its shape.

Can you think of any other **shapes**?

circle **triangle** **star** **square**

share

When you share something, you give part of it to someone else.

Flynn didn't think he'd have to **share** this feast with Pascal!

sharp

Something that is sharp has a pointed tip or an edge that can cut.

Captain Hook's sword is long and **sharp**.

shark

A shark is a large fish with a big mouth and a fin on its back.

Bruce is a **shark** with a big, toothy grin.

shave

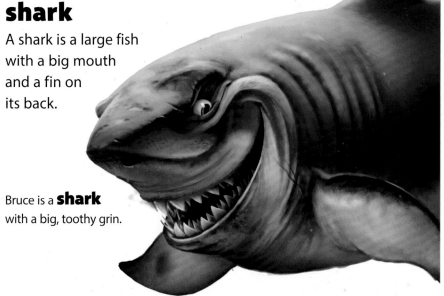

When a man shaves, he uses a razor to trim the hair on his face.

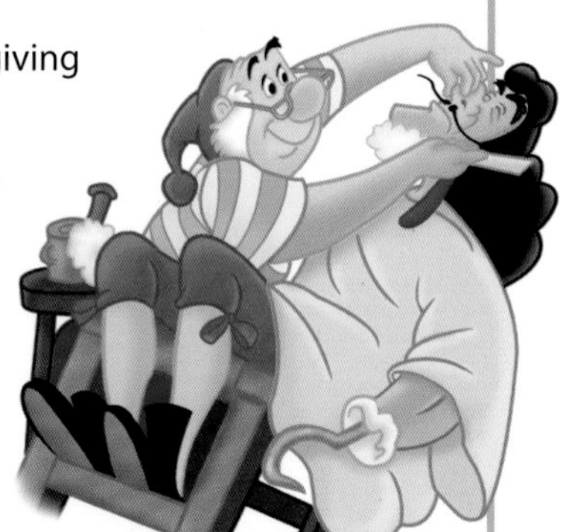

Smee is giving Hook a **shave**.

sheep

Sheep are animals with four legs and curly fur called wool. They say, "Baa, baa!"

Every spring, the **sheep** have their wool sheared.

shell

A shell is a hard covering that protects things like eggs, turtles, clams and nuts.

Moana carefully lifts up the **shell**.

shirt

A shirt is an item of clothing with arms, a collar and buttons down the front.

Bob is wearing a white **shirt**.

sheet

A sheet is a thin, flat piece of cloth that covers your bed.

The birds pull up the **sheet** so Snow White can sleep.

shine

If something shines, it gives off light.

Even a diamond ring can't **shine** as brightly as Ray!

shoes

You wear shoes on your feet, over your socks.

Jiminy Cricket always keeps his **shoes** clean and smart.

shelf

A shelf is a place where you can store things.

Watch out! The ball might roll off that **shelf**.

ship

A ship is a large boat.

The pirate **ship** rocks on the ocean waves.

shop

A shop is a place where you can buy the things you need.

Judy's **shop** is very quiet today.

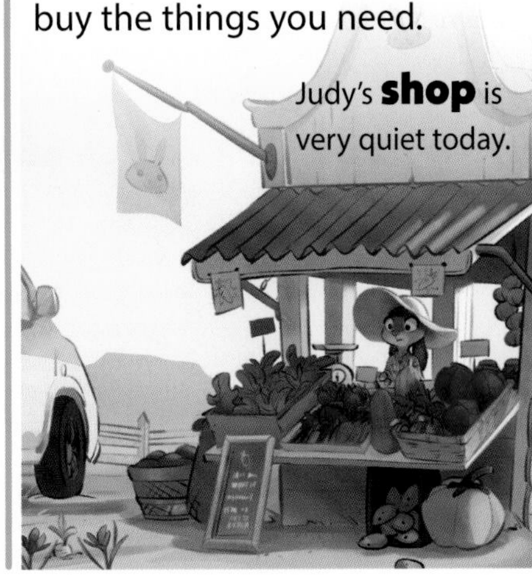

short

Short means not long or tall.

Compared to Nick, Judy is rather **short**!

show

When you show people something, you point it out to them.

Wreck-It Ralph has something to **show** his friends.

shorts

Shorts are trousers that only come as low as your knees.

Andy likes to wear **shorts** when he plays outside.

shower

You stand under a shower to wash yourself with a steady stream of water.

The **shower** is on.

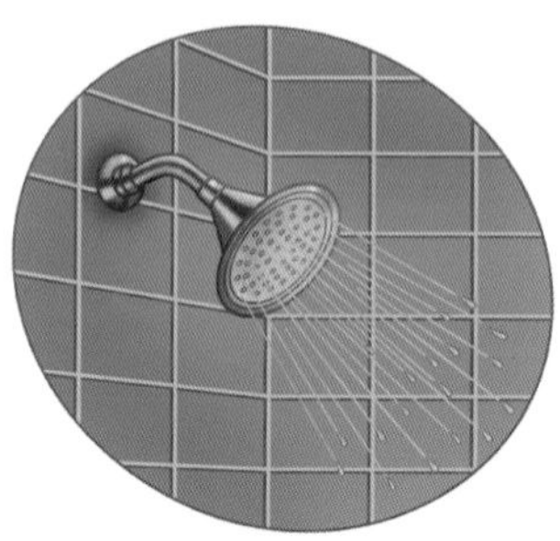

shut

When you shut something, you close something that was open.

Lightning is **shut** inside the scrapyard.

shout

When someone shouts, they call out or yell in a very loud voice.

Rapunzel has never heard Mother Gothel **shout** so loudly!

shy

A shy person is someone who is quiet around other people.

Can you tell that Bashful is a **shy** dwarf?

sign
A sign contains writing, sometimes with pictures, which has information about something.

This **sign** is pointing to the Snuggly Duckling pub.

singer
A singer is a person who sings.

Tiana is an enchanting **singer**.

sit
When you sit down, you are no longer standing up.

Jasmine wants to **sit** on her own for a while.

sing
When you sing, you make music with your voice.

Ariel loves to **sing** into the sea breeze.

sink
A sink is the bowl in your kitchen or bathroom that the water from the taps runs into.

This **sink** is full of soapy dishes.

skateboard
A skateboard is a long, flat board on wheels that you ride by pushing one foot along the ground.

If you go out on your **skateboard**, put on your safety gear first!

sister
Your sister is the female child of your parents.

Anna would do anything for her big **sister**, Elsa.

ski
To ski means to come down a hill on long boards called skis.

Mickey is trying to **ski** as fast as he can.

skip
When you skip, you move by jumping and hopping along, one foot at a time.

Jasmine wants to **skip** for joy!

skyscraper
A skyscraper is a very tall building with many floors.

You will usually find a **skyscraper** in a big city.

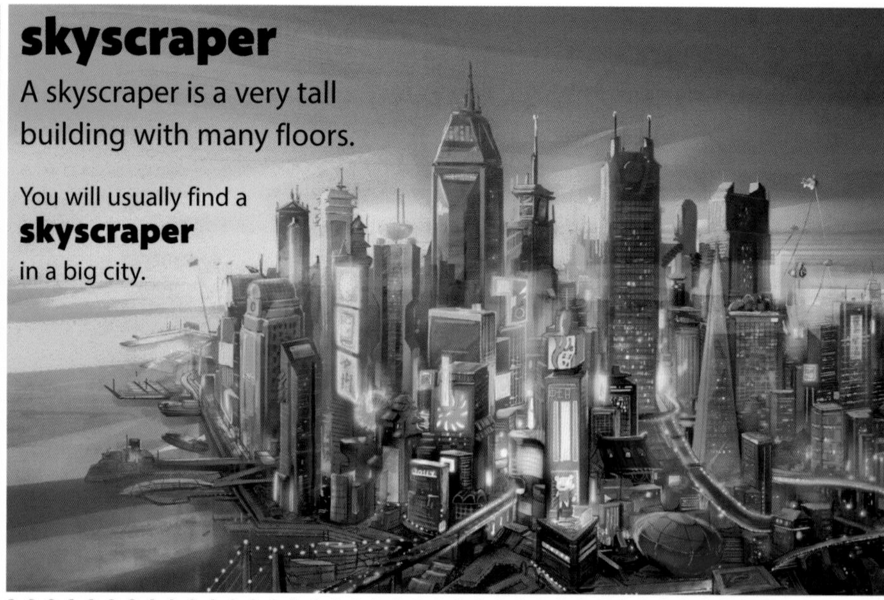

skirt
A skirt is a piece of clothing that begins at the waist and falls around the legs.

A **skirt** can be short, knee-length or long.

sledge
A sledge is a flat board with blades underneath that you sit on to ride down snowy hills.

A **sledge** can slide very fast down a steep hill.

sleeping bag
A sleeping bag is a warm, padded bag that you zip yourself into when you're not sleeping in a bed.

In the mountains, everybody needs a warm **sleeping bag**.

sky
The sky is what you see when you are outside and look up.

Look at the beautiful colours in the **sky**.

sleep
When you sleep, you relax with your eyes closed, stop moving and thinking, and begin dreaming.

Goodnight, **sleep** tight!

slice
A slice is a small portion that has been cut from a bigger piece of food.

Would you like a **slice** of broccoli pizza?

slide
A slide is something that you slip down, usually on your bottom.

Elsa and Olaf watch Anna **slide** down the frozen stream!

slow
Slow is the opposite of fast.

Lizzie used to be speedy, but now she is rather **slow**.

smell
When you smell something, you use your nose to inhale its scent to learn about it.

Belle can **smell** the rose's sweet perfume.

small
If something is small, it doesn't take up much space.

It doesn't matter if you are **small**, you can still be mighty!

smile
A smile occurs when you are happy and your mouth turns up at the corners.

Joy likes to **smile** every single day.

slippers
Slippers are soft shoes that you wear at home, usually when you're in your pyjamas.

Geppetto always wears a pair of warm **slippers**.

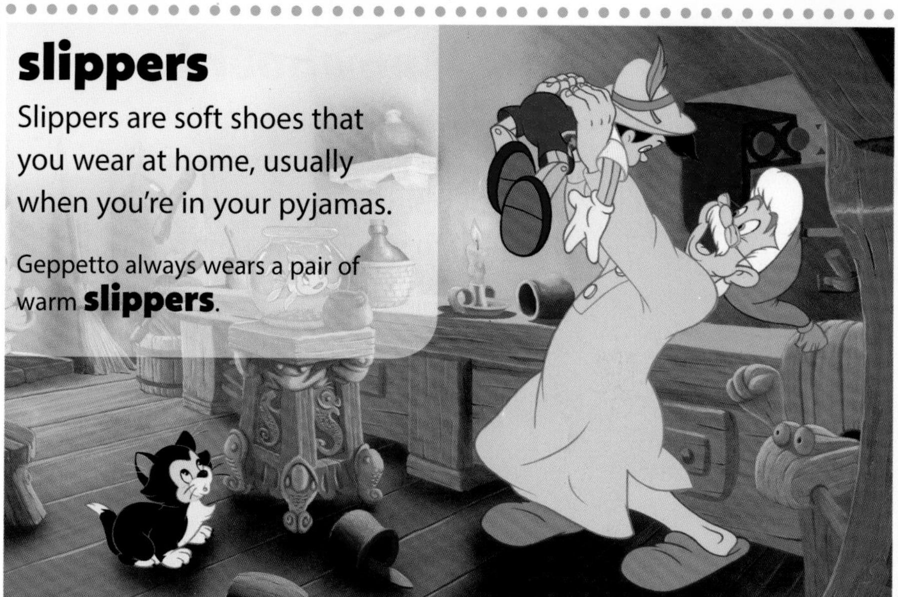

smoke
Smoke is the cloud that rises from something burning.

Grey **smoke** billows above the forest fire.

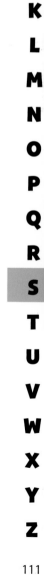

snack

A snack is something you eat between meals.

Pooh helps himself to a **snack**.

snake

A snake is a long, thin reptile that has no legs and slithers along the ground.

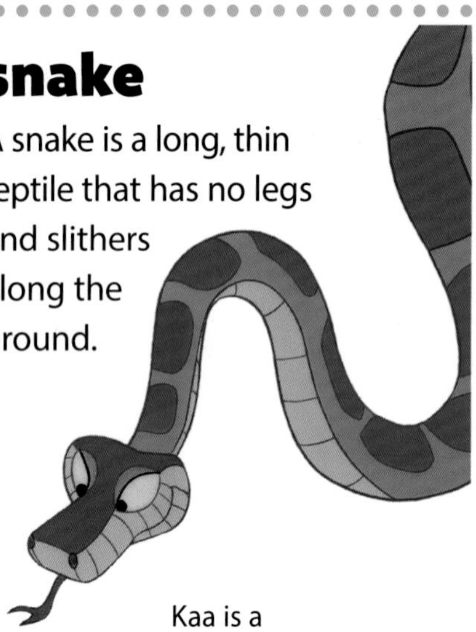

Kaa is a slithery **snake**.

sneeze

When you sneeze you make a noise as a lot of air suddenly comes out of your nose and mouth.

Uh-oh! Another **sneeze** is on its way!

snow

Snow is made up of white flakes of ice that sometimes fall from the clouds in cold weather.

Arendelle is covered in a carpet of **snow**.

snowball

A snowball is a round ball of snow, made to throw.

Anna and Elsa are having a **snowball** fight.

snowboard

A snowboard is a flat piece of fibreglass or plastic that someone stands on to slide down a snowy hill.

Mickey is testing out his new **snowboard**.

snowflake
A snowflake is a single piece of snow. No two snowflakes are exactly alike.

A **snowflake** shower is magical to see.

socks
Socks are items of clothing you wear on your feet, under your shoes. Socks come in pairs.

The workers at Monsters, Inc. can be freaked out by human **socks**.

someone
Someone means some person.

Baloo wants **someone** to dance with him.

snowman
A snowman is made when big balls of snow are shaped to look like a person.

Olaf is a merry little **snowman**.

sofa
A sofa is a long, soft piece of furniture that goes in your living room.

A **sofa** is a comfy place to sit and watch TV.

somersault
A somersault is an acrobatic movement which involves a flip in the air.

Hud is performing an awesome **somersault** on the race track!

soap
Soap is what you use when you wash. It can smell nice and helps to make you clean.

Grumpy has slipped on this bar of **soap**.

soft
When something is soft, it feels fluffy to touch.

Art is very proud of his **soft**, purple fur.

son

A son is the male child of his parents.

Marlin crossed the ocean to find his **son**, Nemo.

song

A song is when words are put together and projected by your voice to make a tune.

Cinderella's morning **song** would melt even the hardest heart.

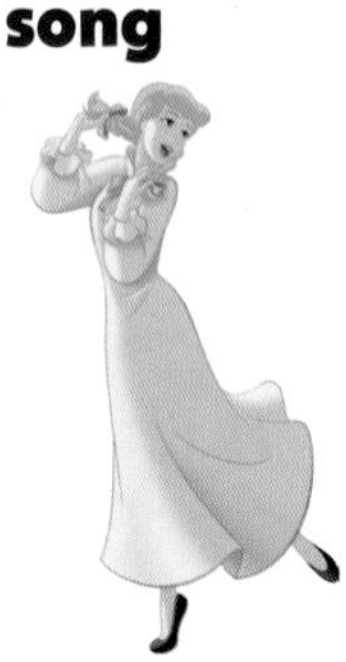

soup

Soup is a hot liquid food made with water or milk and other things, such as meat and vegetables.

Hot **soup** tastes great on a cold winter's day.

soon

If something is going to happen soon, it means it will happen a short time from now.

Lightning hopes that his race will be starting **soon**.

south

South is the direction that is the opposite of north.

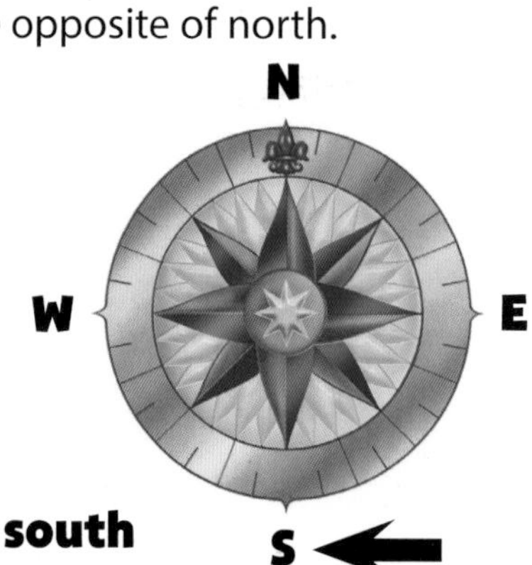

The **south** is always towards the bottom on a map.

space

Space is everything that exists beyond our planet Earth.

Buzz is an intergalactic **space** ranger.

spaceship

A spaceship is a machine, powered by a rocket motor, that travels into space from the Earth.

Many humans can travel inside this vast **spaceship**.

spade
A spade is a tool with a handle and a scoop, used for digging.

A bucket and **spade** are useful when you're on the beach.

spider
A spider is a small animal that has eight legs and spins webs.

Rosie is a black widow **spider**.

spinach
Spinach is a dark green, leafy vegetable.

Spinach leaves are good for you.

spoon
A spoon has a little scoop at the end of a handle and is used for eating soft or wet things.

You eat soup with a **spoon**.

spot
A spot is a small mark on something.

Little Pua has a dark **spot** over one eye.

spring
Spring is one of the four seasons. In spring it rains a lot and flowers start to grow.

Olaf is full of the joys of **spring**!

squirrel
A squirrel is a small, furry animal with a bushy tail, that lives in trees and eats nuts.

A **squirrel** likes to store food for the winter.

stable
A stable is a place where farm animals are kept.

The **stable** door is open, so the animals can listen!

stadium

A stadium is a place with many seats around an open space in the middle, where people go to watch sports or music events.

Dusty Crophopper zooms through the **stadium**!

start

When you start something, you begin to do it.

Poor Nanny doesn't know where to **start**!

stage

A stage is a raised area in a theatre where actors, musicians and dancers perform in front of an audience.

Hiro takes his place on the **stage**.

stand

To stand means to be up on your feet.

Pocahontas likes to **stand** by the peaceful river.

station

A station is a place where people go to catch trains, buses or coaches.

Judy says a sad goodbye at the railway **station**.

stamp

A stamp is a small piece of paper that people stick on a letter or package in order to post it.

Make sure that you put a **stamp** on your letter!

star

A star is a twinkling light, made up of gases, that you can see in the night sky.

Every **star** in the sky makes the night a little brighter.

stay

To stay somewhere means to remain there.

Poor Lightning has to **stay** like this until someone comes to help.

stone

A stone is a small piece of rock.

Each little blue **stone** in the tank needs to be kept clean.

stop

When you stop doing something, you don't do it any more.

Woody wants Bullseye to **stop** licking his ear!

story

A story is a tale with a beginning, a middle and an end. It could be true or make-believe.

Belle wants to read you a **story**.

stepmother

A stepmother is a woman who marries your father after his marriage to your mother ends.

Snow White's **stepmother** is a wicked woman.

storm

A storm is a kind of weather with rain or snow and usually a lot of wind.

Dusty is trying to fly through the **storm**.

A B C D E F G H I J K L M N O P Q R S T U V W X Y Z

strange

Something that is strange is unusual and different.

Some monsters can look rather **strange**.

street

A street is the road that cars drive along.

Mater has stopped in the middle of the **street**.

straw

A straw is a long narrow paper or plastic tube that you use to drink something.

Suck in your cheeks when you drink through this **straw**.

stretch

When you stretch, you spread your arms, legs and body out to full length.

Rapunzel can **stretch** her arms out wide!

stripe

A stripe is a line of colour.

Tigger thinks a **stripe** or two might look nice on Eeyore!

strawberry

A strawberry is a small, red fruit with lots of seeds. It grows close to the ground.

A fresh **strawberry** tastes juicy and sweet.

string

String is a narrow, thin rope.

Merida pulls back the **string** on her bow.

strong

If someone is strong, they have a lot of power.

Gaston has big, **strong** muscles.

student

A student is someone who is attending a school, college or university to learn a particular subject.

Mike can't wait to be a **student** at Monsters University.

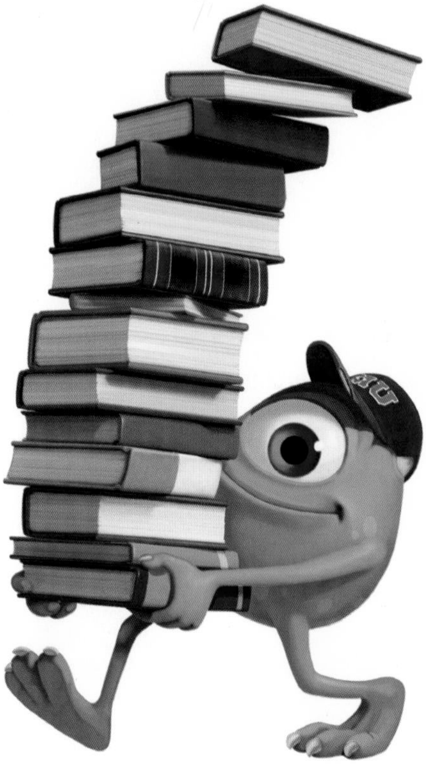

suit

A suit is a matching set of clothes such as trousers or a skirt paired with a jacket.

Mayor Lionheart always goes to work in a **suit**.

sun

The sun is a star that sends light and heat to Earth.

The **sun** rises up above the mountaintops.

suitcase

A suitcase is a container with a handle that people pack their clothes in when they travel.

What is inside that **suitcase**?

sunbathing

Sunbathing means to stay out in the sun.

Olaf dreams of **sunbathing** on a sandy beach!

sugar

Sugar is a white or brown food that makes other food taste sweeter.

Sugar comes in grains or cubes.

summer

Summer is one of the four seasons. It is the hottest and sunniest time of year.

Olaf thinks **summer** might be the best season of all!

sunglasses

Sunglasses are glasses that you wear to protect your eyes from too much sunshine.

Would you like to pick a pair of **sunglasses** from Minnie's stand?

sunset

Sunset is the time of day when the sun goes down.

At **sunset**, the dinosaurs must find somewhere to shelter for the night.

sunrise

Sunrise is the time of day in the morning when the sun comes up.

The animals are up at **sunrise** every day.

sunscreen

Sunscreen is a liquid you put on your skin to protect it from being burned by too much sunshine.

Before you sit in the sun, you must put on lots of **sunscreen**.

surfboard

A surfboard is a plastic board that people stand on while riding ocean waves.

You need to balance just right on a **surfboard**.

supermarket

A supermarket is a big shop that sells all sorts of different foods and household objects.

There's a brand new **supermarket** in town!

surfing

Surfing means to ride on a surfboard in the sea.

Lilo has been going **surfing** ever since she was tiny.

surprised

If you are surprised by something, it means you weren't expecting it.

Ariel is **surprised** to see a set of wiggly toes!

swimsuit

A swimsuit is the piece of clothing you wear when you go in the water.

Lilo has a striped **swimsuit**.

sweater

A sweater is a knitted piece of clothing you wear to keep warm.

Squishy is proud of his Oozma Kappa **sweater**.

swim

When you swim, you move through the water, using your hands and feet.

Moana loves to **swim** through the ocean.

swing

A swing is a seat that swings from ropes. You sit on it and pump your legs up and down.

An old tyre on a rope also makes a good **swing**.

sweet

Something tastes sweet if it has sugar or honey in it.

Officer Clawhauser is eating a **sweet** doughnut.

sword

A sword is a weapon with a handle attached to a long piece of metal with sharp edges.

Mulan holds her **sword** like a true warrior.

Tt

table
A table is a piece of furniture with a flat top and legs to hold it up.

Merida's little brothers sit up at the **table**.

tablet
A tablet is a small, handheld computer.

Mickey reads the news on his **tablet**.

tail
A tail is something some animals grow at the lower end of their backs.

Sven's **tail** is short and twitchy.

take
To take something means to get possession of it.

Ursula casts a spell to **take** Ariel's voice.

talk
When you talk, you say words out loud.

A candlestick cannot usually move and **talk**!

tall
When someone is tall, there is a long distance from their feet to their head.

Vanellope has never met anyone quite as **tall** as Wreck-It Ralph!

tambourine

A tambourine is a musical instrument you hit. It also has metal discs around the edges that jingle when you shake it.

Bang the **tambourine** in time to the beat!

tea

Tea is a hot liquid that people drink, made with water and the dried leaves of certain plants.

Mrs Potts serves up a wonderful cup of **tea**!

teapot

A teapot is a container with a handle and a spout in which you make and serve tea.

Mrs Potts is a very fine china **teapot**.

taste

When you taste something, you put it into your mouth to see what flavour it is and whether you like it.

Merida wants her mother to **taste** the cake.

tear

When something tears, it is pulled apart.

In stormy seas, rocks and stones can **tear** at your clothes.

taxi

A taxi is a car driven by a taxi driver, who people pay to drive them somewhere.

A **taxi** has a meter to tell you what the fare will be.

teacher

A teacher is someone who helps you to learn new things.

Professor Knight is a **teacher** at Monsters University.

teddy bear

A teddy bear is a stuffed animal in the shape of a bear.

Lotso is a strawberry-scented **teddy bear**.

A B C D E F G H I J K L M N O P Q R S T U V W X Y Z

telephone

A telephone is a machine that lets you talk to someone who is not in the same place as you.

Nick has got a message on his **telephone**.

temper

If you have a temper, it means you have trouble controlling your anger.

Extra homework puts Sulley in a bad **temper**.

tent

A tent is an outdoor shelter made of strong cloth and poles.

Goofy has almost finished putting up his **tent**.

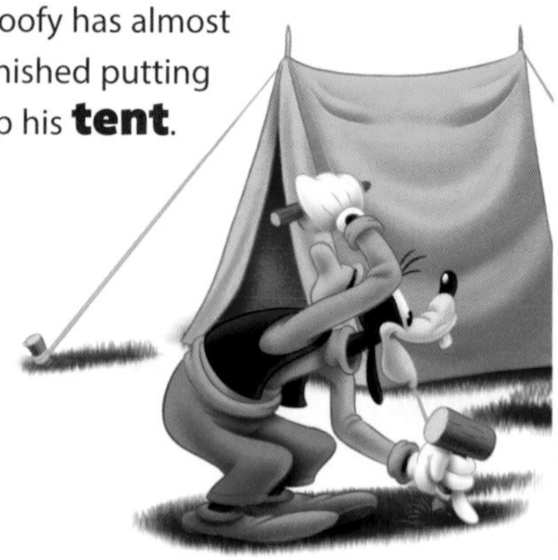

television

A television, or TV, picks up sounds and pictures that are broadcast for entertainment or information.

The dalmatians gather around the **television**.

test

When you take a test, you answer questions to show how well you know something.

Chief Bogo sets a **test** for the new recruits.

tell

When you tell someone something, you are sharing information that you know.

Ariel wishes she could **tell** the prince that she loves him.

tennis

Tennis is a game where players hit a tennis ball back and forth over a net with a tennis racket.

Can you spot the **tennis** racket?

text message

A text is a written message you send and receive using a mobile phone.

You can send a **text message** to tell someone when you will arrive.

thermometer

A thermometer is something that measures the temperature of a person or a place.

This glass **thermometer** has liquid inside.

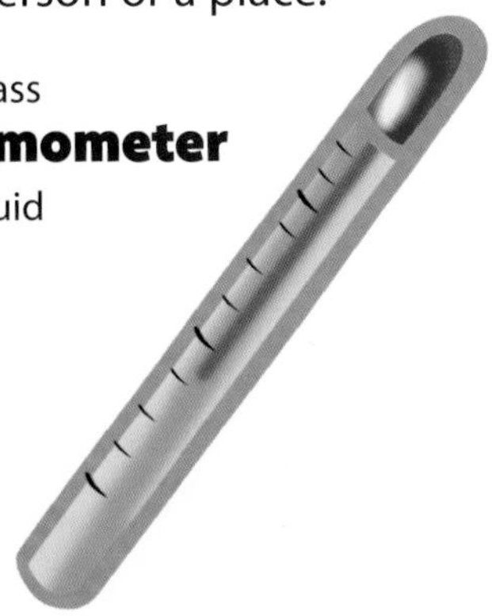

think

When you think, you use your mind to form an idea or plan.

Gill asks Nemo to **think** about his plan.

thick

When something is thick, it is not thin.

Baymax's body is as broad as it is **thick**.

thirsty

If you are thirsty, it means you need something to drink.

Moana is tired and **thirsty**.

throw

When you throw something, you use your hands to make it fly through the air.

Mickey can **throw** the Frisbee right across the park.

thin

A thin person is someone who has very little fat on their body.

Peter Pan is nimble and **thin**.

through

Through means from one end to the other.

Hank is able to squeeze **through** the smallest spaces.

thunder

Thunder is the loud noise that comes from the sky soon after you see lightning.

The **thunder** roars above the castle.

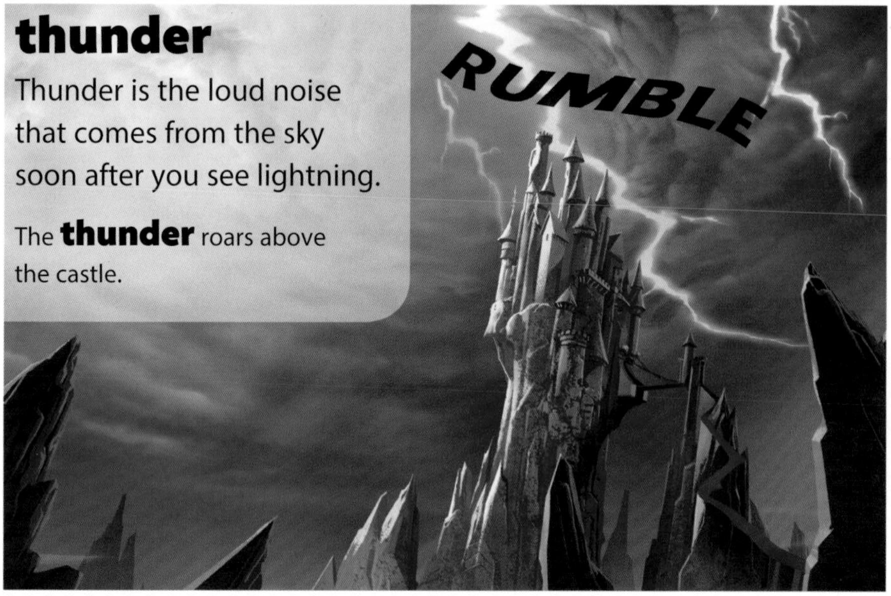

time

Time is how long it takes for something to happen. Time is also the hours and minutes on a clock that show where you are in your day.

Cogsworth always knows the right **time**.

ticket

A ticket is a piece of paper that you buy in order to go somewhere.

You need a **ticket** to travel on the bus.

tie

To tie something means to hold it together. A tie is also an item of clothing you wear around your neck.

You **tie** a **tie** around your neck!

tin

Metal cans are made of tin.

This **tin** holds tomatoes.

tidy

When you are tidy, it means that you are neat and orderly.

Let's **tidy** up these pots and pans!

tiger

A tiger is the largest wild cat. It has orange or white fur and dark stripes.

Jasmine likes to pat and hug her pet **tiger**, Rajah.

tired

You are tired if you are sleepy or need to rest.

The king and queen are very **tired**.

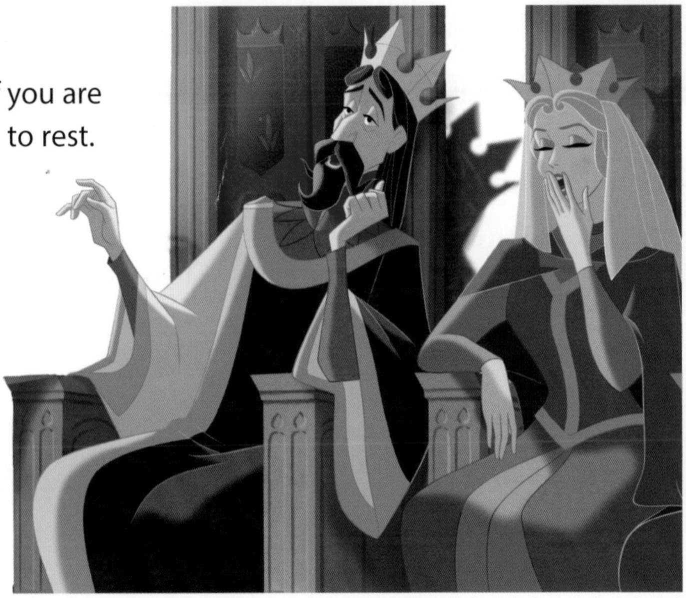

together

Together means with someone or something.

Ariel and Flounder explore the ocean **together**.

tissues

Tissues are soft pieces of paper you use to wipe something with.

You wipe your nose with **tissues** when you have a cold.

toaster

A toaster is an electric machine that heats bread to turn it into toast.

This **toaster** can toast two slices of bread at one time.

toilet

A toilet is a bowl with water that you use to flush away your body's waste.

You'll find the **toilet** in the bathroom!

toast

Toast is bread that has been heated in a toaster until it is brown and crunchy.

The **toast** pops up when it's ready.

today

Today means this day.

Mike starts at Monsters University **today**!

tomato

A tomato is a bright red fruit that grows on a vine and has seeds.

A sliced **tomato** is good in sandwiches and salads.

tomorrow

Tomorrow is the day after today.

Maurice won't be back until **tomorrow**.

toothpaste

You put toothpaste on your toothbrush to help clean and polish your teeth.

Monsters use lots of **toothpaste** when they brush their teeth!

torch

A torch is an object with a bulb and batteries that makes a beam of light.

A **torch** can help you see in the dark.

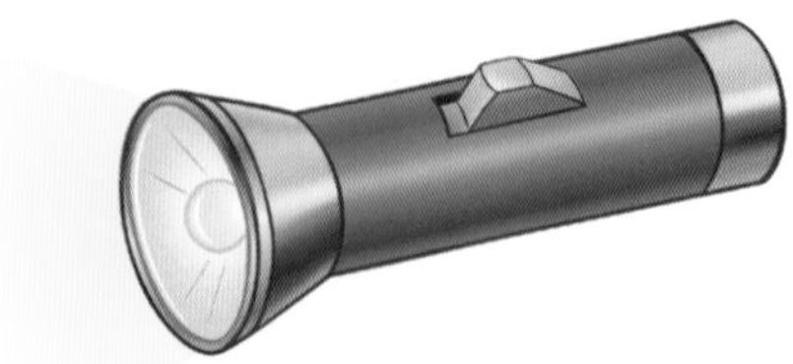

tonight

Tonight means later today, when the afternoon has ended.

Tonight is the night that Cinderella will go to the ball!

tortoise

A tortoise is an animal that lives on land and moves very slowly.

A **tortoise** has a shell on its back.

toothbrush

You brush your teeth with a toothbrush.

If you go to a sleepover, don't forget your **toothbrush**.

top

The top of something is the very highest part of it.

Tinker Bell gazes up to the **top** of the winding road.

touch

When you touch something, you use your hand to feel it.

The lamp is dull and cold to **touch**.

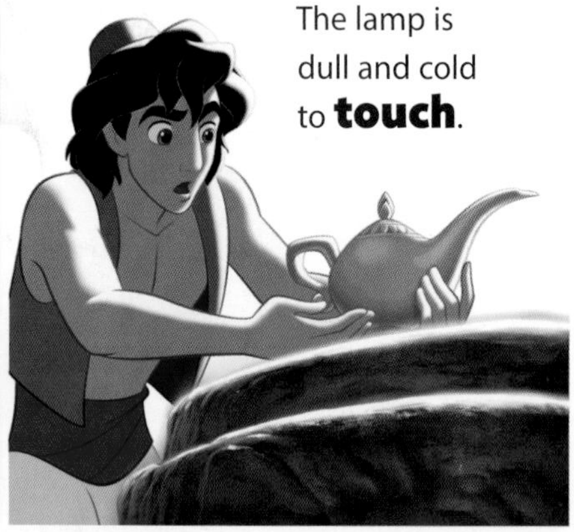

towel
A towel is a thick piece of cloth that you use to dry things.

Aladdin wobbles above a **towel** on a washing line.

town
A town is place where people live and work. It is bigger than a village, but smaller than a city.

Arendelle **town** is so pretty in the winter.

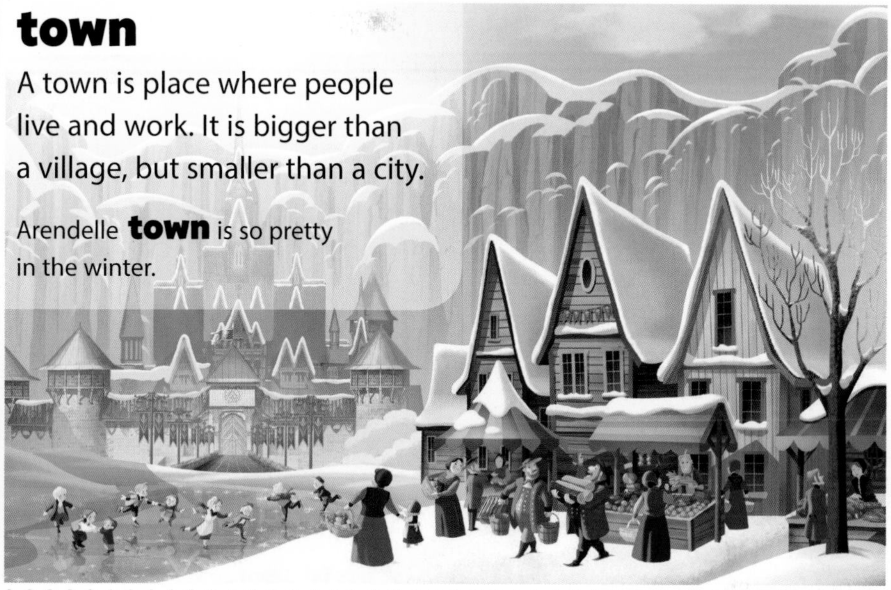

tower
A tower is a very tall, thin building.

Rapunzel lives in a lonely **tower**.

toy
A toy is something you play with, such as a doll or ball.

Rex is a **toy** dinosaur.

tractor
A tractor is a big machine used to pull farm machines or heavy loads.

Mater likes to go out **tractor** tipping!

toy box
You keep your favourite toys in a toy box.

This **toy box** is full to the brim!

traffic
Traffic means all of the cars, trucks, buses and other vehicles that are on the road at one time.

During rush hour, there can be a lot of **traffic**.

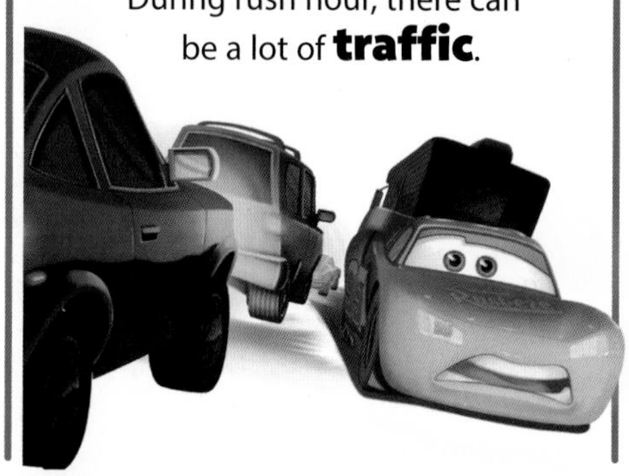

train

A train is a vehicle with an engine at the front, which pulls lots of carriages along a railway track.

The circus **train** puffs along the track.

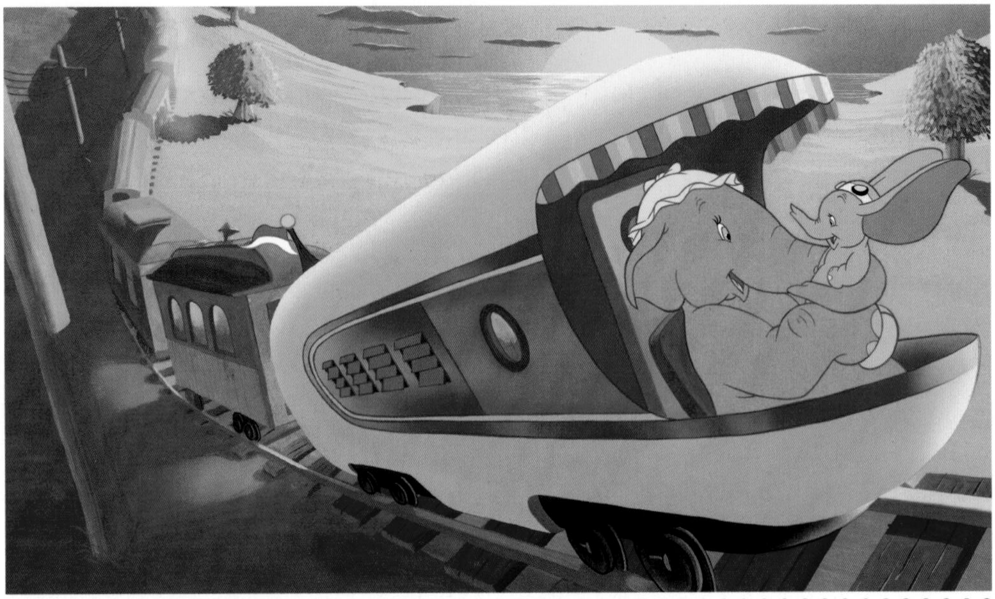

trainers

Trainers are shoes with rubber bottoms and soft tops.

The Hamada brothers wear **trainers** most of the time.

treasure

Treasure is a collection of valuable things.

Prince John wants to steal the king's **treasure**.

tree

A tree is a large and very tall plant with deep roots, a trunk and branches.

A fir **tree** is green all year round.

tray

A tray is a flat piece of metal, wood or plastic on which you carry things.

Tiana can carry a **tray** in each hand.

trip

When you take a trip, you go somewhere else, for a holiday or for work.

Anna is going on a **trip** with Kristoff and Sven.

truck

A truck is a big vehicle that carries heavy loads from one place to another.

Mack is a tired **truck** tonight!

trophy

A trophy is an award you get for doing well in some sport or other event.

Lightning dreams of winning a **trophy** of his own.

trumpet

A trumpet is a musical instrument made of brass, with only three keys.

When you blow a **trumpet**, a loud sound comes out.

turn

When you turn something, you move it in a different direction or in a circle.

A magic carpet can flip and **turn** in the air.

trousers

Trousers are what you wear on the lower part of your body to cover your legs and bottom.

Watch out, Jasper! Your **trousers** might fall down!

twins

Twins are two people born at the same time to the same mother and father. Some twins look exactly alike.

Tweedledee and Tweedledum are identical **twins**.

Uu

ugly
Something that is ugly is unpleasant to look at.

The old witch looks **ugly** and strange.

umbrella
An umbrella is a piece of material on a handle that you open to keep rain from getting you wet.

This **umbrella** looks rather small!

uncle
Your uncle is the brother of your father or mother.

Simba's **uncle** is sly and cruel.

under
When something is under something else, it is below it.

Who could be hiding **under** these traffic cones?

understand
If you understand something, you know what it means.

Do the children **understand** that they must stay in the reef?

uniform
A uniform is a special kind of clothing that shows what someone's job is, such as a police officer or firefighter.

Judy puts on her **uniform** before she goes to work.

up
When something goes up, it goes from a lower to a higher place.

Carl's house floats **up** into the air!

Vv

vegetable

A vegetable is a plant or part of a plant that you can eat. Cabbage, beans and carrots are vegetables.

A carrot is a **vegetable** that you pull out of the ground.

vet

A vet is a doctor who takes care of animals.

Daisy Duck is learning how to be a **vet**.

video game

A video game is a game you play on a special video game player.

You can play a **video game** on your own or with friends.

violin

A violin is a musical instrument with four strings that you play with a bow.

Every orchestra has a **violin**.

visit

When you visit, you go somewhere to see someone or something.

Anna and Kristoff have come to **visit** the trolls!

voice

Your voice is the sound of you talking and singing.

The Beast never tires of hearing Belle's **voice**.

volleyball

Volleyball is a game played by two teams where each team hits a ball over a net with their hands.

Donald is a **volleyball** champ!

A B C D E F G H I J K L M N O P Q R S T U V W X Y Z

Ww

waiter/waitress

A waiter or waitress takes your order and serves you food and drink in a restaurant.

Tiana works as a **waitress**.

wake up

When you wake up, you are no longer asleep.

The Dwarfs have been waiting for Snow White to **wake up**!

walk

When you walk, you move by placing one foot in front of the other.

Belle goes for a **walk** through the countryside.

wallet

A wallet is a flat, folded container in which you keep money, photographs and other things.

This **wallet** has got bank notes inside it.

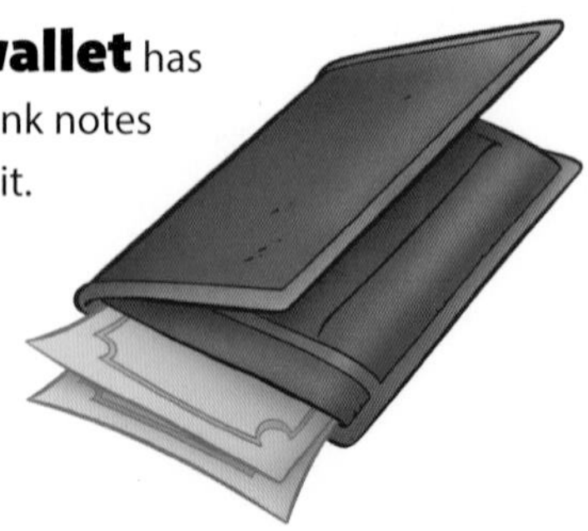

wardrobe

A wardrobe is a big cabinet that holds clothing.

Daisy Duck's **wardrobe** has run out of space!

warm

When you are warm, you are feeling quite hot.

Anna isn't used to this **warm** weather!

warn

When you warn someone you tell them that something bad is going to happen.

The animals of the forest are trying to **warn** the dwarfs!

wash

When you wash something, you use water, and maybe soap, to clean it.

Lightning wasn't expecting to have a **wash** today!

washing machine

A washing machine uses water and electricity to wash clothes.

A **washing machine** is good for clothes, not trucks, silly!

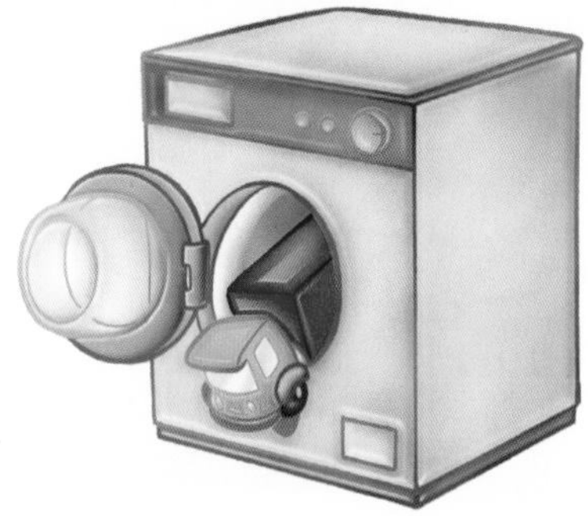

watch

A watch is a small clock you wear around your wrist.

This **watch** has got a gold strap.

water (action)

When you water a plant or a lawn, you pour water on it to help it grow.

It's time for Winnie the Pooh to **water** the flowers.

water (liquid)

Water is the clear liquid that comes from rain, melting snow or oceans, rivers and lakes.

Maui and Moana look out across the **water**.

waterfall

A waterfall is a wide stream of water that falls from a high to a low place.

The **waterfall** makes a lovely gushing sound.

A B C D E F G H I J K L M N O P Q R S T U V W X Y Z

watermelon

A watermelon is a large fruit with a green peel and juicy, red insides with lots of seeds.

Yum! **Watermelon** is a sweet summer snack.

week

A week is seven days – Monday, Tuesday, Wednesday, Thursday, Friday, Saturday and Sunday.

Some people write their plans on the calendar every **week**.

west

West is the direction that is the opposite of east. On a map, west is on the left side.

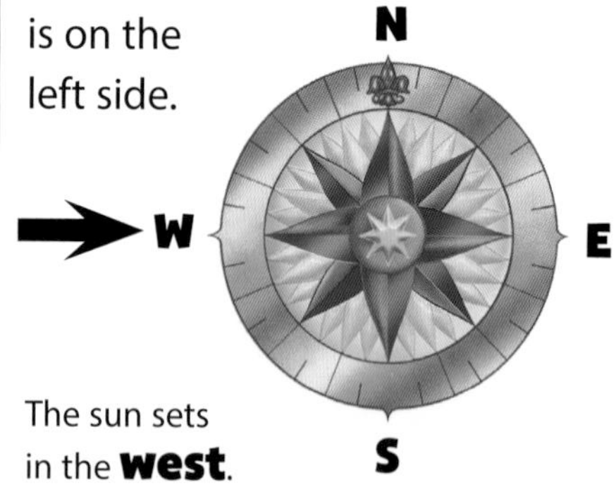

The sun sets in the **west**.

wave

When you wave at someone, you move your hand from side to side to say hello or goodbye.

Bing Bong likes to **wave** when he spots a friend.

weekend

Saturday and Sunday are the two days which make up the weekend.

Mickey and Minnie are spending the **weekend** with Donald Duck.

wear

To wear something means to be dressed in some sort of clothing.

Cinderella can't wait to **wear** this pretty pink dress!

weigh

How much things weigh means how heavy or light they are.

That tree trunk must **weigh** a lot!

wet

When something is wet, it means it has water in it or on it.

Gaston does not like getting his hair **wet**!

whale
A whale is the largest animal that lives in the sea.

A **whale** swims up to the surface to breathe.

whisper
When you whisper, you talk in a very quiet voice, so that only the person you are talking to can hear you.

Merida likes to **whisper** in Angus's ear.

whole
If something is whole, it means it is all there and that none of it is missing.

Do you think that you could eat a **whole** pizza?

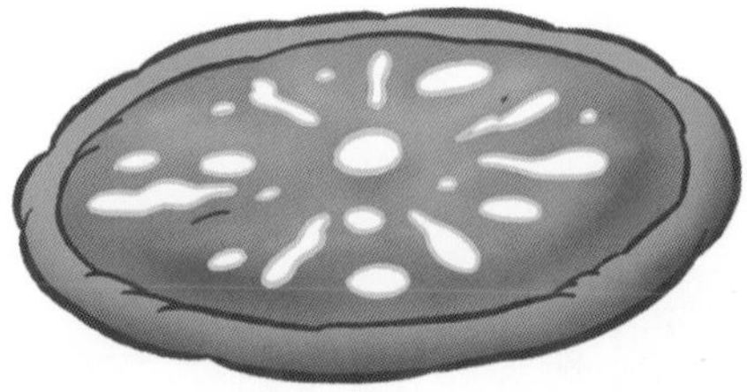

wheel
A wheel is a circular object that can turn around.

A **wheel** with a thick tyre is better at gripping the road.

whistle (object)
A whistle is a small instrument that makes a loud sound when you blow into it.

Coaches use a **whistle** when they teach football.

wide
If something is wide, it takes up a lot of space from side to side.

The entrance to Monsters University is tall and **wide**.

wheelchair
A wheelchair is a special chair that helps people who are unable to walk.

A **wheelchair** has four wheels.

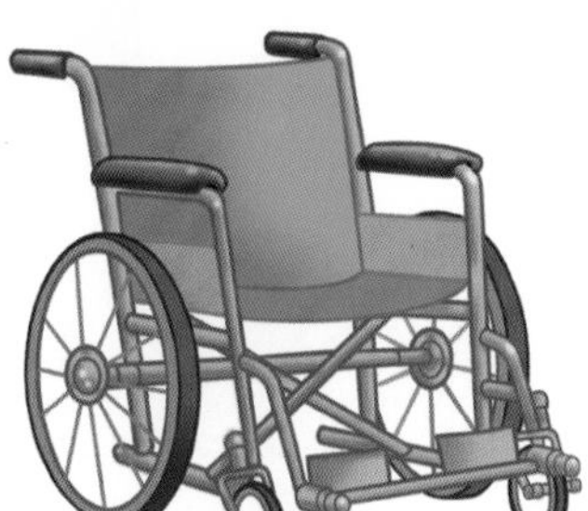

whiteboard
A whiteboard is a hard surface that can be written on, then wiped clean again.

Someone has drawn a happy picture on this **whiteboard**!

wife
A wife is a woman who is married.

Carl loves his **wife** Ellie very much indeed.

A B C D E F G H I J K L M N O P Q R S T U V W X Y Z

win

When you win a contest or a game, it means that you come in first.

Mike always knew that his team could **win** the Scare Games!

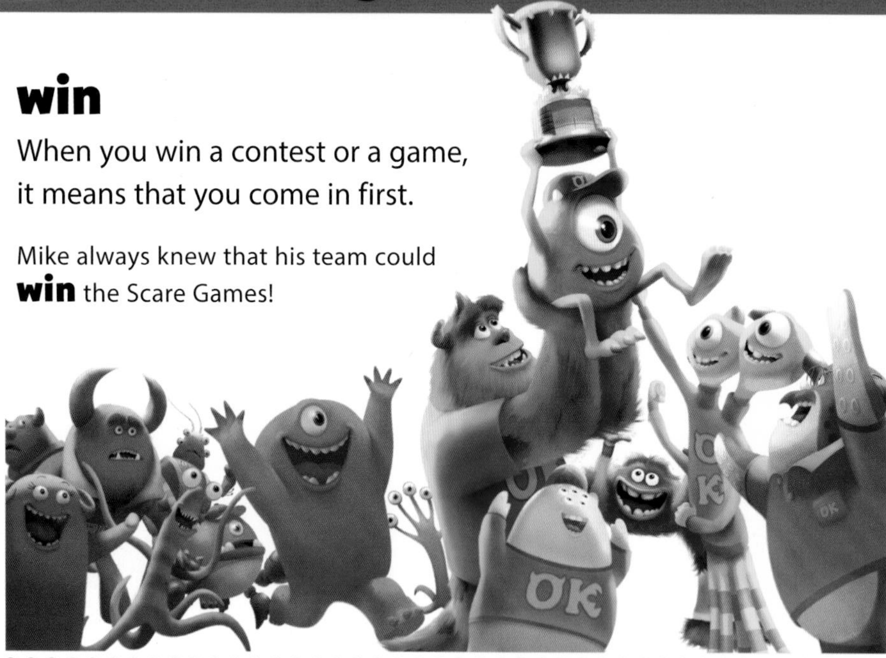

woman

When a girl grows up, she becomes a woman.

Queen Elinor is a proud and strong **woman**.

wind

Wind is air that you can feel when it is moving fast.

The **wind** is very blustery today!

winter

Winter is one of the four seasons. The weather in winter is cold and it has the shortest days.

Winter in Arendelle is a magical season.

wing

A wing is the part of a bird, insect or aeroplane that helps it to fly.

Dusty has a **wing** on each side of his body.

wolf

A wolf is a wild animal that looks like a large dog and howls in the night.

This **wolf** is covered in shaggy fur.

wood

Wood is something you build things with. It comes from the trunk and branches of a tree.

Merida's throne has been carved out of **wood**.

A B C D E F G H I J K L M N O P Q R S T U V W X Y Z

work

Work is the kind of job you do.

The Dwarfs march to **work** every single morning.

worst

Worst is the opposite of best.

Rapunzel thinks this could be the **worst** dress she has ever had to wear!

write

When you write, you make the shapes of letters and words for other people to read.

If she spots something unusual, Judy has to **write** it down.

wrong

If something is wrong, it is not correct.

This is the **wrong** foot for the glass slipper!

A B C D E F G H I J K L M N O P Q R S T U V W X Y Z

Xx

X-ray
An X-ray is a photograph of the inside of someone's body.

This **X-ray** shows how bones fit together.

xylophone
A xylophone is a musical instrument made of strips of metal that you hit to make different sounds.

An undersea **xylophone** makes wobbly, watery music!

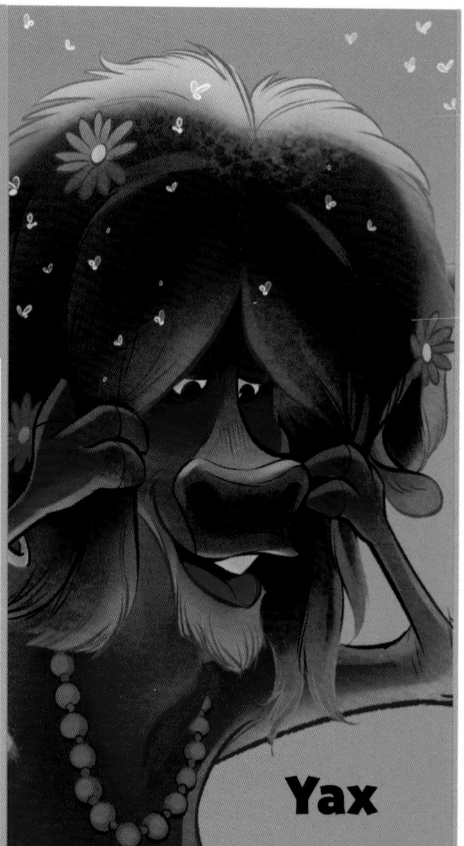

Yy

yawn
You yawn when you are sleepy by opening your mouth wide and slowly breathing in and out.

Owl tries not to **yawn**, but it is past his bedtime!

year
A year is 365 days or 52 weeks or 12 months long.

This calendar shows one whole **year**.

yes
When you say yes, it means you agree with something.

When Bob proposed to Helen, she said, "**Yes**!"

yesterday
Yesterday was the day just before today.

Tiana did not look like this **yesterday**!

yoghurt
Yoghurt is a soft food made from milk that comes in many flavours.

Yoghurt is creamy and delicious.

young
When someone is young, it means they have only been alive for a short time.

Ever since she was **young**, Judy has wanted to be a police officer.

yoga
Yoga is a type of exercise which helps you keep relaxed.

Rafiki is practising his **yoga** poses!

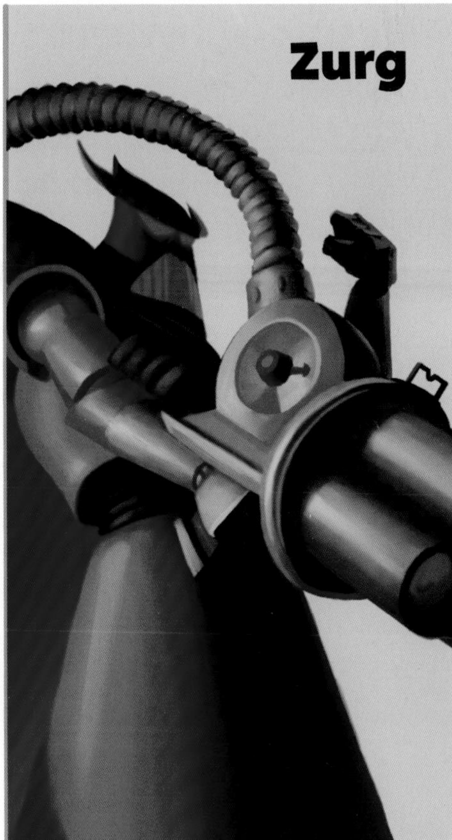

Zz

zebra
A zebra is a wild animal that looks like a horse with black-and-white stripes.

These **zebras** live on the plains of Africa.

zero
Zero is the number for nothing.

Zero comes before one.

zip
A zip has two rows of metal or plastic teeth that fit together when the zip is closed and come apart when it is open.

The **zip** on this jacket has been pulled up to the top.

zoo
A zoo is a place you can visit where all kinds of wild animals live and are taken care of.

Let's take a trip to the **zoo**!